Launch into Literacy

Book 2

Jane Medwell
Maureen Lewis

OXFORD
UNIVERSITY PRESS

Contents

There is no time limit on the sessions and teachers will want to exercise their own skill and judgement when planning

= whole class work

NLS planning chart

	Genre focus	Range of texts	Text features	Reading skills

UNIT·1	TERM 1
	Writing to express:
	    poems on a theme
		poems on the theme of travel
		descriptions
			verses/verse structure
			rhyme
			repetition
			alliteration
			imagery
				literal and inferential
				   comprehension
				   questions
				using a thesaurus
				reading aloud

UNIT·2	TERM 1
	Writing to inform:
	  factual recounts
	  newspaper reports
		historical recount
		newspaper reports
		diary
		time lines
			openings
			conclusions
			chronological order
			key facts
			facts and opinions
				literal and inferential
				   comprehension
				   questions
				using a dictionary
				using a time line
				reading aloud to partner

UNIT·3	TERM 2
	Writing to entertain:
	  science fiction and
	  fantasy
		story beginnings
		science fiction
		fantasy novels
		graphic novels
		descriptions
			narrative openings
			setting/characters/plot
			descriptive language
			events
			evidence/conclusions
			suspense
			clichés
			similes
				literal and inferential
				   comprehension
				   questions
				comparing characters
				using a dictionary
				reading aloud to partner

UNIT·4	TERM 2
	Writing to explain:
	  explanations
		explanations
		annotated diagrams
		leaflets
		tickets
			opening question
			brief answer
			details
			cause and effect
			  statements
			logical relationships
			paragraphs
				literal and inferential
				   comprehension
				   questions
				using a dictionary
				reading non-prose
				  information
				reading aloud to partner

UNIT·5	TERM 3
	Writing to persuade:
	  posters and leaflets
		poster
		letters
		list
		chart
			language study
			word play
			main points
			heading
			slogan
			additional information
			formal/informal language
			greeting
			closure
			key points
			non-chronological order
				literal and inferential
				   comprehension
				   questions
				using a dictionary
				reading aloud to partner
				summarizing

Writing skills	Grammar	Punctuation	Words

writing sentences
brainstorming ideas
planning a poem
drafting a poem
revising a poem
	past tense regular and
	   irregular verbs
	verbs
	adverbs
	nouns/proper nouns
	adjectives
		capital letters	rhyming words
			homophones
			alliteration
			similes
			synonyms
			category and collective
			   nouns
			comparatives

writing sentences brainstorming key facts planning a time line drafting a factual recount revising a factual recount	nouns verbs conjunctions clauses personal pronouns adverbs	commas	definitions root words abbreviations

completing a chart
planning a story
writing descriptions –
   setting
writing descriptions –
   character
drafting a story
revising a story
	adjectives
	regular comparative and
	   superlative adjectives
	irregular comparative and
	   superlative adjectives
	nouns
			similes
			old-fashioned words
			word change
			definitions
			gender words
			comparatives and
			   superlatives
			suffixes
			words indicating degrees
			   of intensity

labelling a diagram extending sentences brainstorming key facts writing notes drafting question and answer drafting an explanation revising an explanation remodelling prose	conjunctions possessive apostrophe plural possessive apostrophe suffixes word function adjectives adverbs	possessive apostrophe plural possessive apostrophe	definitions technical words
completing a chart writing slogans and headings writing a letter listing ideas drafting a poster editing a poster designing poster layout	contractions sentences questions/commands apostrophe of omission pronouns verbs/imperatives connectives	apostrophe of omission question marks full stops bullet points commas	definitions synonyms formal/informal words rhyme

Writing to express

In this unit you will study poems on the theme of travel. You will look at how poets use language to create ideas and images. At the end of the unit you will plan, draft and write your own poem about travelling.

Travel poems

Many Ways to Travel   *by Tony Mitton*

There are many ways to travel
And one that I like
Is to zoom down a hill
On a mountain bike.

There are many ways to travel
And another that is nice
Is to slide on a sledge
On the snow and ice.

There are many ways to travel
And isn't it fun
To sail on the sea
In the wind and sun?

There are many ways to travel
But the best by far
Is to ride on a rocket
To a distant star.

How does this opening catch your interest?

What do you notice about the start of each verse?

What do you notice about these phrases?

What do you notice about these words?

30

- What are the poems about?
- Who is talking in each of the poems?
- Is the action taking place now, yesterday or tomorrow?
- Do all the lines rhyme?
- Why do both poems repeat some lines or phrases?
- How many different ways of travelling are mentioned?

Travel poems

How does this opening catch your interest?

Travelling to School   *by John Coldwell*

If the playground was a runway,
I would fly to school by plane.
If the staff room was a station,
I would steam to school by train.
If the classroom was a stable,
I would ride in at a trot.
If the main hall was a harbour,
I would sail to school by yacht.
But it's just an old brick building
With an iron gate,
And if I don't start running,
I'm going to be late.

What do you notice about these words?

31

5

Looking closely at the poems

1 Read the **poems** 'Travelling to School' and 'Many Ways to Travel' again. Answer these questions about the poems.

   a Tony Mitton thinks the best way to travel is
      to sail?   to zoom on a bike?   to ride on a rocket?

   b Sledges   *slide?   zoom?   sail?*

   c In John Coldwell's poem the child really travels to school   *by train?   on foot?   in a yacht?*

   d What will happen to the child if he does not start running?

   e List five different vehicles for travelling mentioned in the poems.

> There are many words in the poems that **rhyme**.
> The ends of words which rhyme sound the same when we say them.
> EXAMPLE: n**ice** and **ice**
> They do not have to be spelt the same.
> EXAMPLE: pl**ane** and tr**ain**

2 Complete this chart. Find the rhyming words in the poems and then add any other rhymes you can think of. The first one has been done for you.

Word from the poem	Rhyming word in the poem	Other rhyming words
like	*bike*	*pike, spike, Mike, dyke*
nice		
fun		
far		
trot		
plane		
gate		

3 Chose some words from one of your completed rows. Use them to make up a silly **sentence**.
   EXAMPLE: Mike's bike has a pike on a spike.

Same but different: homophones

Homophones are words that sound the same but have different meanings or different spellings.

EXAMPLE: **plain** – something without decoration

plain – a flat area of grassland

plane – a machine that flies through the air

1 Here are some words from the **poems** on pages 4 and 5. There are also some homophones of these words. Match each word with its correct **definition**.

Word
sail
sale
main
mane
sea
see

Definition
the hair on a horse's neck
the most important thing
to view something
salt water covering much of planet Earth
a piece of cloth used to make a yacht move
an event where objects are sold at a reduced price

SAIL SALE   SAIL SALE

2 Think of the homophones for these words from the poems:
star, train, stable.
Write two definitions
for each word.

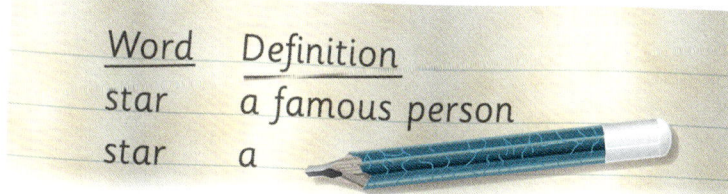

Word	Definition
star	a famous person
star	a

We need to be careful
not to mix up homophones when we are writing.

wear ware where

there they're their

two too to

Remember
You might need to check the meaning in a dictionary.

3 Choose one of the words to complete each **sentence**.
   a I walk ____ school.
   b Sailors ____ a life-jacket when they go sailing.
   c ____ are many ways to travel.

4 Now make up three sentences about travelling using a word from each of the sets of homophones above.

Glossary
poem
definition
sentence

Breaking the rules: irregular verbs

We add -ed to the end of most **verbs** to make the **past tense**. These are **regular verbs**. Some verbs have their own rules. These are called **irregular verbs**.

EXAMPLE: **Present tense**   **Past tense**

I jump   I jumped   (regular verb)

I see   I saw   (irregular)

1 Decide which of these past tense verbs is correct.

    a I runned   or   I ran

    b I swimmed   or   I swam

    c I goed   or   I went

    d I thinked   or   I thought

    e I eated   or   I ate

    f I travelled   or   I trove

2 Now use the correct verbs from the list above to complete this passage.

3rd August

Last week I ____ on holiday to Spain. I ____ by plane. I ____ the hotel was great. It had a swimming pool so I ____ every day. I ____ some great Spanish food called paella. When we got home my dog was waiting for me and I ____ to give him a big hug.

3 Reread the **poems** on pages 4 and 5. These verbs are from the poems: fly, steam, sail, run, zoom, slide, ride. Complete this chart. The first one is done for you.

Verb	Past tense	Regular/Irregular verb?
steam	steamed	regular
fly		
sail		
run		
zoom		
ride		
slide		

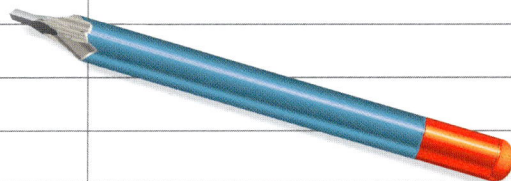

8

Using sounds: alliteration

Reread the **poem** 'Many Ways to Travel' on page 4.
Then look again at the third line in each **verse**.

> Did you notice that in verses 2, 3 and 4 the
> **verbs** and the **nouns** begin with the same letters?
> EXAMPLES: **s**lide on a **s**ledge   **r**ide on a **r**ocket
> When several words begin with the same **consonant**
> we call this **alliteration**. **Poets** often use alliteration as
> a way of emphasizing words.

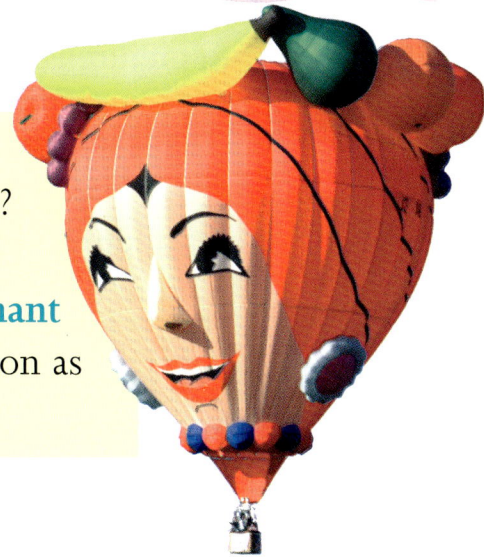

1 Write an alliterative line for line 3 in verse 1.
   Is to h _____ down a hill

2 Write an alliterative verb
   for these ways of travelling.
   EXAMPLE: to *bounce* on a bus
   a to r _____ on my rollerblades
   b to s _____ on a surfboard
   c to c _____ in a car
   d to b _____ in a balloon

3 We can also use alliteration when we are adding
   adjectives. Add two alliterative adjectives to each
   of these nouns.
   EXAMPLE: bus – *a battered, blue bus*
   a rollerblades
   b surfboard
   c car
   d balloon

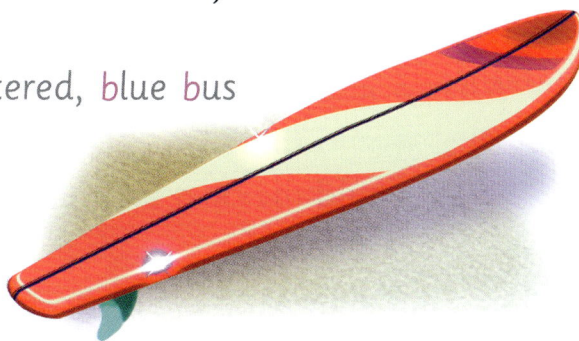

4 Write your own alliterative **sentence**
   describing how you travel to school.

> **Remember**
> You can use
> alliteration when
> you write your
> own poem.

> *Glossary*
> poem
> verse
> verb
> noun
> consonant
> poet
> adjective
> sentence

Powerful words

You are now going to look closely at another travel **poem** and see how the choice of words helps to create pictures in our minds.

In this poem the **poet** uses the human senses – touch, taste, sight, smell – to describe what it would be like to have wings.

Travel poems

Wings *by Pie Corbett*

If I had wings
    I would touch the fingertips of clouds
        And glide on the wind's breath.

If I had wings
    I would taste a chunk of the sun
        As hot as peppered curry.

If I had wings
    I would breathe deep and sniff
        The scent of raindrops.

If I had wings
    I would gaze at the people
        Who cling on to the earth.

If I had wings
    I would dream of
        Swimming the deserts
            And walking the seas.

1 Read the poem and answer these questions.
   a What would the poet see?
   b What would the poet taste?
   c What would the poet smell?
   d What would the poet touch?

2 Write a **verse** saying what the poet might hear when he was flying.

If I had wings
I would hear . . .

Text features:
imagery
Reading skills:
comprehension
Words:
similes

Poets often compare something to something else to make a vivid picture for the reader.

EXAMPLE: '**as hot as** peppered curry'

This way of comparing one thing with another is called a **simile**.

3 Write a simile for each of these travelling **verbs**. Use either 'as' or 'like'. The first two have been done for you but you can also write your own simile for these two.

 a glide like a swan on water
 b run as fast as an Olympic sprinter
 c fly
 d zoom

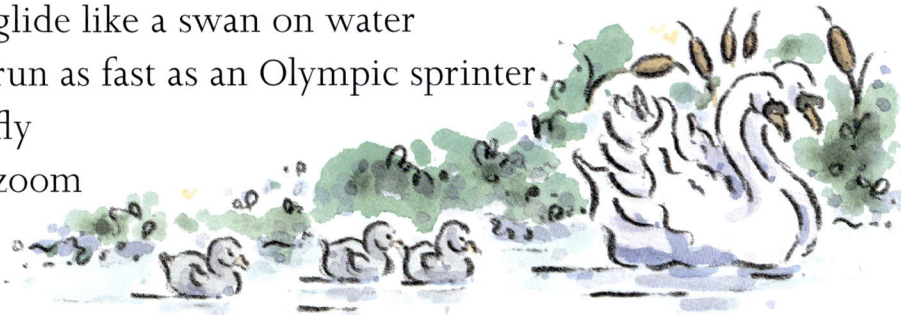

Remember

You can use similes when you write your own travel poem.

Sometimes poets use their imagination to describe something that does not actually exist.

EXAMPLE: 'the fingertips of clouds'

Or they might describe something we could not actually do.

EXAMPLE: 'walking the seas'

These surprising ways of describing things can help the reader create a picture in his or her mind.

4 Find three more surprising things in the **poem** that are created by the poet's imagination.

 a the wind's
 b the   of raindrops
 c   the deserts

5 Write your own surprising image for these travelling verbs.
 a sailing the ...   b riding ...

Glossary

poet
verb
poem

UNIT·1 **Writing to express**

Reading skills:
using a thesaurus
Words:
synonymous verbs
synonymous
adjectives

More powerful words: synonyms

1 Reread the **poem** 'Wings' on page 10.

The **poet** does not use the **verb** 'look'. He uses the word 'gaze'. There are lots of verbs that mean the same as **look**. EXAMPLES: **stare**, **peep**, **glance**, **see**, **ogle** Words which have similar meanings are called **synonyms**. Choosing just the right synonym can make a piece of writing more vivid. It would be boring to just use 'look' all the time.

2 List all the words you can think of that you could use instead of these verbs: walk, fly.

3 Choose a verb from each list. Write a **sentence** and draw a picture to accompany it.

Concorde flashed across the sky.

He dawdled to school.

A thesaurus is a book which helps you find words which are synonyms. It is arranged alphabetically, like a dictionary.

dawdle   58

dawdle *Don't dawdle: we haven't got all day.* to be slow, to dally, to hang about, to lag behind, to linger, to straggle.
dawn day-break, sunrise.
dazed *The blow dazed him.* amazed, bewildered, confused, shocked, stunned.

deb
h
to
tl
c

dec
h'

Glossary

poem
poet
verb
sentence
adjective

4 Think of all the synonyms you can for these **adjectives**.
   a beautiful – *pretty, stunning, …*
   b huge – *big, enormous, …*
   c clever – *brainy, …*

5 Now check your list using a thesaurus.

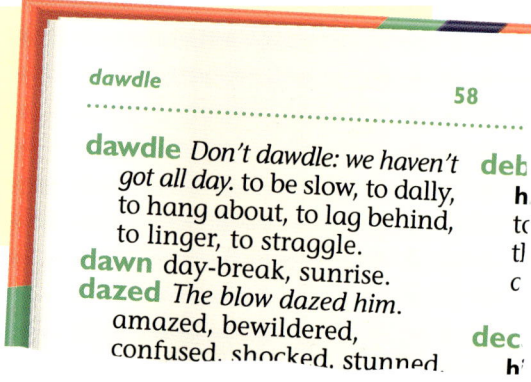

UNIT·1 Writing to express

Words:
simile
alliteration
Grammar:
proper nouns
Punctuation:
capital letters

From a Space Rocket *by Raymond Wilson*

We looked back at the World
    rolling through Space
like a giant Moon with a calm
    cool silver face.

All its cities and countries
    had faded from sight;
all its mountains and oceans were turned
    into pure light.

Slowly, its noise and troubles
    all seemed to cease,
and the whole World was beauty and silence
    and endless peace.

1 Read the **poem** to yourself two or three times. Think about what it means. Now complete these **sentences**.
  a A **simile** in the poem is ...
  b There is **alliteration** in the words ...
  c A surprising image is ...
  d In each verse, lines 2 and 4 ...

Proper nouns

In this poem some words have **capital letters** to make them stand out. EXAMPLES: **S**pace, **M**oon, **W**orld
Usually, we do not use capital letters unless they are **proper nouns**.

1 Complete this sentence.

Proper nouns are . . .

2 Add capital letters to the proper nouns in this passage.

> apollo 11 landed on the moon on july 20th 1969. The first man to step onto the moon was neil armstrong. The other members of the crew were edwin aldrin and michael collins. The president of the united states of america – richard m. nixon – sent them a message of congratulations.

Glossary
poem
sentence

UNIT·1 Writing to express

Grammar:
proper nouns
Vocabulary:
category nouns
collective nouns

Naming things

1 Reread 'From a Space Rocket' on page 13. Find these words in the **poem**.   cities   mountains

countries   oceans

> Each of the four **nouns** listed above describes a **category** of individual nouns.
> EXAMPLE: **Rome** and **Paris** belong to the category 'cities'.

2 Add five **proper nouns** to each category word above.

3 Think of a category noun that links Mars and Earth. Add more nouns to the category list.

> **Collective nouns** are used to name groups of individual things when they are gathered together.
> EXAMPLE: Instead of 'group' we might say
>   a **shoal** of fish, or a **herd** of cattle.

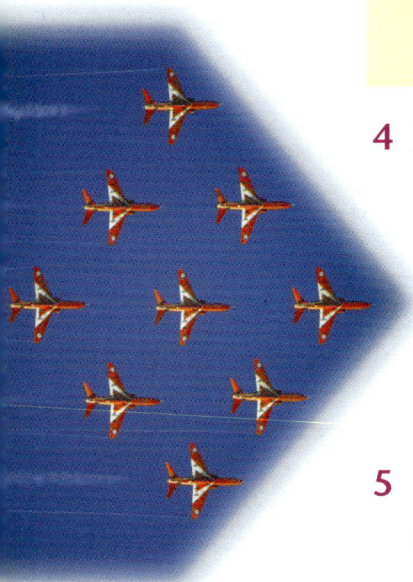

4 Match these collective nouns to their objects.
   a flotilla of ...
       a school of ...   wolves
         a pack of ...   ships
      a swarm of ...   fighter planes
   a formation of ...   dolphins   bees

5 Now make up your own collective nouns for:
   a a ___ of rockets   **b** a ___ of planets   **c** a ___ of buses

Travel poems

Far Trek   *by June Brady*

Some things will never change although
We tour out to the stars;
Arriving on the moon we'll find
Our luggage sent to Mars!

Fast or faster: comparatives

This **poem** describes what travelling at speed is like.

From a Railway Carriage *by Robert Louis Stevenson*

Faster than fairies, faster than witches,
Bridges and houses, hedges and ditches;
And charging along like troops in a battle,
All through the meadows the horses and cattle:
All of the sights of the hill and the plain
Fly as thick as driving rain;
And ever again, in the wink of an eye,
Painted stations whistle by.

31

1 Read the poem to yourself. Think about what it means.

> Some words can be used to compare things.
> EXAMPLE: 'Faster than ... Faster than ...'
> 'Faster' is a **comparative**. We make most comparative
> **adjectives** and **adverbs** by adding -er. Sometimes we
> put 'more' in front of a word when making a comparison.
> EXAMPLE: Trains are **more exciting** than cars.
> Not Trains are excitinger than cars.

Here are some more words we might use to describe travelling.

thrilling quick smooth
boring noisy slow

2 Use some of the words above to complete these
  sentences. You will have to turn them into comparatives.
  a A canal barge is   than a speed boat.
  b You get a   ride on inflated tyres than flat tyres.
  c A flight on Concorde is   than a flight
     on a jumbo jet.

3 Use three remaining words from the list in three
  sentences about travel. Turn them into comparatives.

Remember
You can use
comparatives
in your poem.

Glossary
poem
adjective
adverb
sentence

Writing a travel poem

You have looked at several travel poems in this unit. Now you are going to write your own poem about travelling.

Brainstorm

1 Reread the travel poems on pages 4 and 5.

2 Brainstorm all the different ways of travelling and different means of transport you can think of.

car

ride

horse

ways of travelling

swing

balloon

fly

glider

sail

3 Decide which of your ideas you will use from your brainstorm and say more about them. You will have lots of sentences. Some you will use in your poem, some you will discard.

Plan

I fly on the park swing

Flying on the swing I see the ~~clouds~~ ~~trees~~ people

On the swing I dream of flying

4 Work on the language of each of the sentences you have written. Play around with lots of different ideas.

- Try adding alliteration.
- Try adding similes.
- Try adding adjectives, adverbs.
- Use 'strong' verbs.
- Try using each sense to give a structure to your poem.
- Try using the same opening line for each verse.

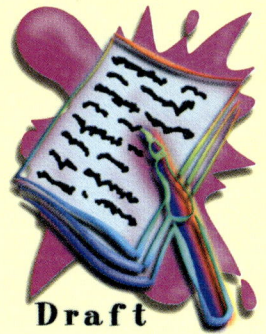

Draft

5 Now write a first draft using the sentences you like best.

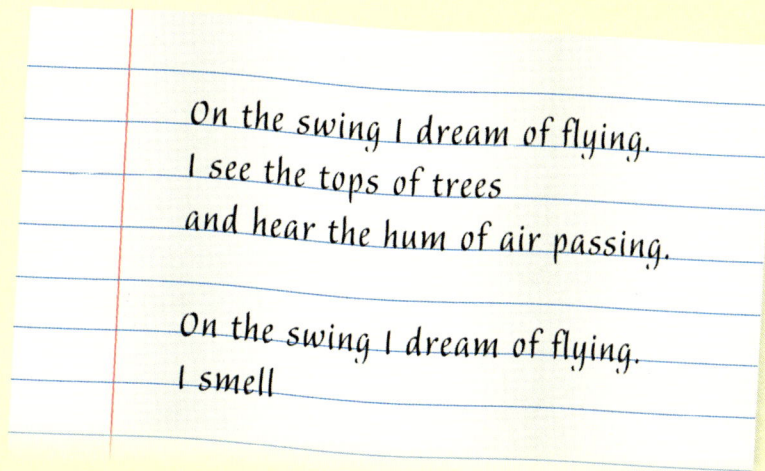

> On the swing I dream of flying.
> I see the tops of trees
> and hear the hum of air passing.
>
> On the swing I dream of flying.
> I smell

6 Swap your first draft with a friend. Ask them which parts they think are good and why, and whether there are any parts they don't like.

Revise

7 Make any alterations that will improve your poem.

8 Copy out your final draft and display it. You could use a piece of mounting paper shaped like a plane or a rollerskate, or anything else to do with travel.

9 Have a poetry-reading session when you read your poems aloud to each other.

Publish

17

Writing to inform

In this unit you will study how to write a factual recount. You will look at how factual recounts contain key information and often tell events in order. At the end of the unit you will plan, draft and write your own factual recount.

The Voyage of HMS Endeavour

Which important person is named early in the recount?

HMS *Endeavour* set sail from Plymouth on 26 August 1768 with James Cook in command. The ship was only 32 metres long but it had to carry ninety-four men, including some famous scientists. They hoped to sail to the Pacific island of Tahiti. There they would watch the 'Transit of Venus' – the movement of the planet Venus across the Sun. That was the official purpose of the expedition. But James also had some secret orders. He was to search for the Great Southern Continent, which no European had ever found.

What key information is given in the opening few sentences?

It was a difficult voyage for everyone on board. At last, on 13 April 1769 James guided the ship safely into Matavai Bay, Tahiti, in good time for the scientists to see the transit. Luckily the native people of Tahiti were very friendly and James enjoyed getting to know their customs. On 13 July 1769 it was time to move on – into the unknown.

events in order

The *Endeavour* sailed west then south. After three months a large mass of land loomed ahead. It was

10

Here is part of a recount of the life of a famous explorer – Captain James Cook.

- What is the recount about?
- Where is it taking place?
- Is it happening now or a long time ago?
- What are the most important things you learn from this recount?

New Zealand, which had first been seen by Dutch sailors in 1642. Was this a part of a Great Southern Continent? Before James could find out, the local people – the Maoris – made a fierce attack on the *Endeavour*. The crew managed to beat off the Maori war canoes, but they had to stay on constant alert for more attacks. James then took the ship carefully along the coast, making a map as he went. New Zealand turned out to be made up of two islands.

Heading west again, James found another shore and began to map it. One place was so full of new plants he called it Botany Bay (botany is the study of plants). His men also spotted some strange hopping animals – kangaroos. James called this wonderful land New South Wales, because it reminded him of Wales in Britain. Later, it would be known as Australia. Eventually the *Endeavour* sailed back home to England. The expedition had lasted for three years. The voyage had been a huge success. James's report of it made him very famous.

What tense is used?

What do these final sentences do?

from *Captain Cook* by Haydn Middleton

11

UNIT·2 **Writing to inform**

Reading skills:
comprehension
using a dictionary
Vocabulary:
word meanings
Text features:
facts and opinions

Understanding the passage

1 Reread the passage about Captain Cook on pages 18 and 19. Now answer these questions:

   a When did the *Endeavour* leave Plymouth ?

   b In what year did the *Endeavour* return to England ?

   c What did the scientists want to see ?

   d What were Captain Cook's secret orders ?

   e Why do you think it was a difficult voyage ?

   f What are the native people of New Zealand called ?

2 Find these words in the passage. Choose the right meaning. Use a dictionary to check your answers.

   a customs means

   things people do?

   a place that checks what comes into the country?

   b expedition means

   a journey of discovery?   *a boat trip?*

   c alert means

   watchful?   *careless?*   *happy?*

   d native means

   wears special clothes?   *belonging to a country?*

3 Imagine this voyage was to be reported in a newspaper. Make up headline for it.

PLYMOUTH TIMES

JULY 12, 1771.

Crowds cheered and families wept yesterday as HMS *Endeavour* sailed into Plymouth Harbour after

4 Rewrite the first paragraph of the **recount** on page 18 as though it were going in the local paper under your headline. You can add personal details (such as how people felt/looked) and opinions (such as 'I think they are very brave').

Glossary

recount

Events in order

Chronological order is when the order in which events happen follow one after the other. A time line is a way of representing the passing of time.

1 Reread the passage about Captain Cook on pages 18 and 19. Use the chronological information in the passage to complete this time line of the *Endeavour's* journey.

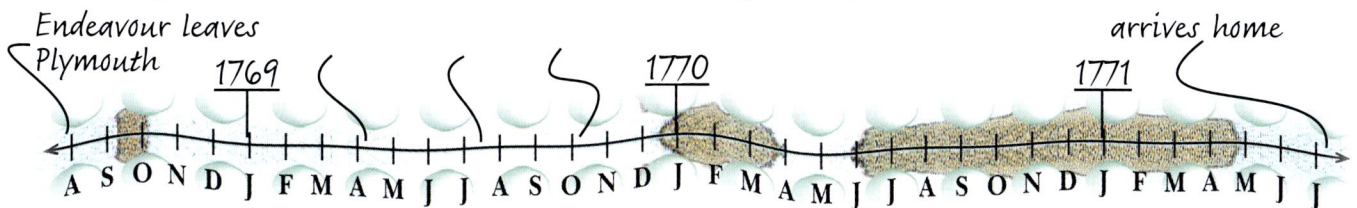

Endeavour leaves Plymouth 1769   1770   1771   arrives home

A S O N D J F M A M J J A S O N D J F M A M J J A S O N D J F M A M J J

Here is a time line of Captain Cook's life.

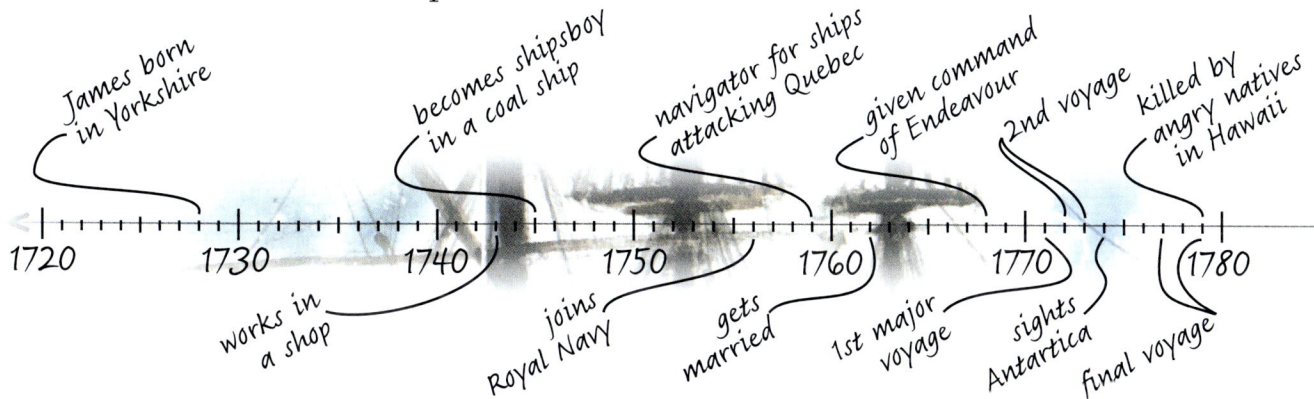

James born in Yorkshire   becomes shipsboy in a coal ship   navigator for ships attacking Quebec   given command of Endeavour   2nd voyage   killed by angry natives in Hawaii

1720   1730   1740   1750   1760   1770   1780

works in a shop   joins Royal Navy   gets married   1st major voyage   sights Antartica   final voyage

2 Use the time line to answer these questions.
   a When and where was James Cook born?
   b When did Captain Cook die?
   c What was his first job?
   d When did he first go to sea?
   e Which was the first ship he commanded?
   f What was James's job in the attack on Quebec?
   g Was James married?
   h How did Captain Cook die?

3 Make a time line of what you did yesterday.

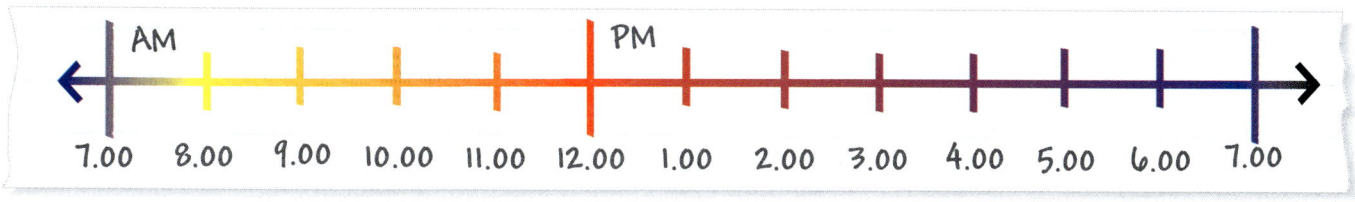

Remember
Make sure your answers are written in sentences.

AM   PM

7.00 8.00 9.00 10.00 11.00 12.00 1.00 2.00 3.00 4.00 5.00 6.00 7.00

Making new words

We can often make new words from a given word.

EXAMPLES: **science – scientist, scientific**
botany – botanist, botanical

Adding -ist to the end of the word or part of the word, often makes a new word, meaning someone who studies that subject.

EXAMPLE: A **scientist** studies **science**.

1 What do these people study? Try to work it out from the word.

a chemist   **b** artist
c biologist **d** herbalist

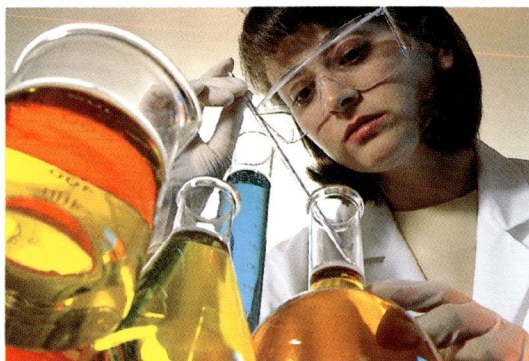

We can also make the name of a job by adding -er to the end of the **verb**. This changes the verb into a **noun**.

EXAMPLE: **verb**   **noun**
            to paint   painter

2 Change these verbs into nouns by adding -er. Put each word into a **sentence**. One has been done for you.

a to teach
b to drive
c to farm
d to clean

I want to be a teacher when I grow up.

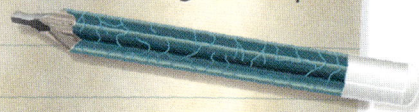

We can also change verbs into nouns by using the word differently in a sentence.

EXAMPLE: I can **swing** my arms. (swing used as a verb)
          I play on a **swing**. (swing used as a noun)

Glossary
sentence

3 Write sentences using these words first as a verb and then as a noun.   drive   drink   sail

Joining sentences

1 Read this **sentence** from the **recount** about Captain Cook.

> Luckily the native people of Tahiti were very friendly
> **and** James enjoyed getting to know their customs.

Conjunctions are the words we use to join sentences together. Conjunctions can be used in the middle or at the beginning of the new sentence.

EXAMPLES: The Tahitians were friendly. The sailors liked them.

Because the Tahitians were friendly the sailors liked them.

The Tahitians were friendly **so** the sailors liked them.

2 Here are some more pairs of sentences about Captain Cook. Join each pair together into one sentence.

a Cook had two sets of orders. One set was secret.

b The *Endeavour* was a small ship. It was crowded.

c The Maoris attacked. The sailors managed to beat them off.

d The ship went to Tahiti. The scientists wanted to watch the 'Transit of Venus'.

*but because
and so*

3 List all the conjunctions in the following passage.

> James spent only a year at home with his family before he set out on another voyage. Again, he was to look for the Great Southern Continent as he had not discovered it on his last journey. He set out in July 1772. James commanded the *Resolution* and Tobias Furneaux was in charge of the *Adventure*. But the further south they sailed the worse the weather became. The ships passed huge icebergs until a great sea of ice blocked the way.

Glossary
sentence
recount

Extending sentences: clauses

1 Read this long **sentence** about Captain Cook.

> Making a map as he went, James took the ship carefully along the coast.

2 Would the sentence still make sense if you crossed out the words before the **comma**?

> The part of the sentence that is left still makes sense on its own. This part is called the main **clause**. The main clause is the most important part of the sentence. The other clause has a **verb**, adds more details but does not make a sentence on its own.
>
> EXAMPLE: Putting my coat on top, I closed my suitcase.
>
> *clause that adds detail*   *main clause*
>
> If there is a clause in front of the main clause they are separated by a comma.

3 Decide whether these sentences need a comma.
  a Looking at the map the driver carefully turned right.
  b She ran down the street shouting as she went.
  c He closed the atlas daydreaming of sailing away.
  d Gasping for air she rose to the surface.
  e Taking careful aim he shot for goal.

Remember
The main clause
should make
a sentence on its
own if you cross
out the rest.

4 Extend these sentences by adding another clause at the beginning or the end.
  a She crossed the road.
  b He drank a milkshake.
  c They saw their friends.

Glossary
sentence
verb

Shortened forms of words

Sometimes we write shortened versions of words or phrases, or we use just the initials, rather than writing something in full. We call these **abbreviations**.

EXAMPLE: **HMS** *Endeavour* written in full would be **H**is **M**ajesty's **S**hip *Endeavour*.

1 Here are some abbreviations based on using initials. Try to find out what they mean. Dictionaries often have lists of abbreviations.

   a BBC   **b** USA   **c** BT   **d** FA

People's titles are often shortened versions of longer words.

EXAMPLES: Mister is written as Mr
           Mistress is written as Mrs
           Sergeant is written as Sgt

Abbreviations used to have full stops after each letter (such as U.S.A.) but nowadays these are usually left out.

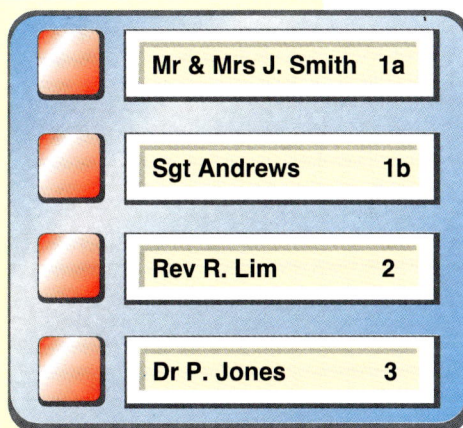

Mr & Mrs J. Smith	1a
Sgt Andrews	1b
Rev R. Lim	2
Dr P. Jones	3

2 What do these abbreviated titles mean?

   a Dr
   b Capt
   c Rev
   d PC
   e John Smith Snr
   f John Smith Jnr

Sometimes we abbreviate our friends' names.

EXAMPLE: Michael – Mike

3 Make a list of all the abbreviated names in your class.

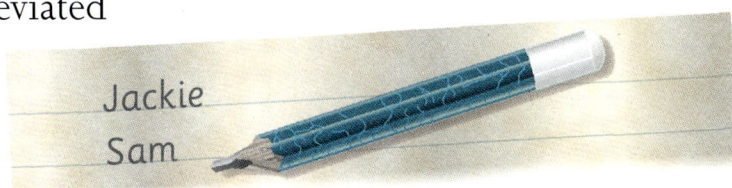

Jackie
Sam

A first person factual recount

You are now going to look closely at a factual **recount** written by someone who took part in the events described.

This is part of the diary of David Hempleman-Adams who walked to the North Pole with Rune Gjeldnes. The diary was printed in the *Daily Telegraph* newspaper.

TUESDAY, MAY 5, 1998

We've made it at last !

The concluding diary of David Hempleman-Adams who, with his companion Rune Gjeldnes, reached the North Pole on April 28

North Pole
Diary

events in order

Day 54: Monday April 27 1998
Walked: 10 miles north
Temp: -32 deg C
Hours of light: 24 hrs

some present tense

WE HAVE camped two miles from the Pole. I hope this is not a mistake. As we get closer we seem to get more worried and confused. The morning started with 25-knot winds and white-out. Cold, especially as I was walking with my trousers torn. All day the wind blew from the east. Hopefully tomorrow the last sprint.

feelings

mainly past tense

Day 55: Tuesday April 28 1998
Walked: to the North Pole
Temp: -35 deg C
Hours of light: 24 hrs

MADE it. Hulashaker! It was still very windy with no sun. It took us one hour to get going, less than usual. We walked for one hour and stopped to plot our position. We turned on our satellite beacon. We sat down and ate some chocolate and had a drink.

One hour later we were walking under a strange, hazy sun. I was enjoying every moment. At 1.12 pm we had half a mile to go. At 1.44 pm we were less than 300 metres from the Pole. Rune paced out to the next stop whilst I filmed the countdown. A great feeling. We stopped for a discussion. Rune wanted me to go first. I wanted us both to go together. Finally went together. The sun was out a little and there was rubble everywhere. I gave Rune a big hug and thanked him. We put the tent up as we were both cold. Thank goodness we made it before the storm came in.

conclusion

Glossary
recount

26

UNIT·2 **Writing to inform**

Reading skills: *comprehension*
Vocabulary: *word meanings*
Grammar: *personal pronoun*

1 Read the diary again and answer the following questions.

   a How were the men travelling?

   b What day of the week did they get to the Pole?

   c Why do you think they both went together for the last few metres?

   d Why do you think there was rubble everywhere at the Pole?

   e What items were the men carrying?

   f Why do you think the same factual information is given at the start of each day?

2 Find these words in the passage from the diary. What do you think they mean?

   a confused

   b white-out

   c paced out

   d position

In the diary **recount** the writer uses the **personal pronouns** 'I' and 'we' because he is writing about himself. In the Captain Cook recount the writer uses the **pronouns** 'he' and 'they' because he is writing about other people, not himself. When somebody writes about themselves we say they are writing in the **first person**.

3 Rewrite the diary entry for Monday as though you were a reporter writing about the men. Use the pronouns 'they' and 'he', not the first person. The newspaper report has been started for you.

Nearly there !

The two men think they have camped

4 What effect does changing the pronouns make?

5 Add a headline to your newspaper report.

Glossary
recount
pronoun
first person

Adding detail to verbs: adverbs

The diary entry on page 26 says,
'Rune paced out to the next stop.'
We have to imagine how he did it.
If it said, 'Rune paced out quickly,'
or, 'Rune paced out carefully,' we would
have a clearer picture of what he did.
'Quickly' and 'carefully' are both **adverbs**.
Adverbs give more detail about the **verb**.
Many adverbs are formed by adding -ly
to the end of other words.

1 The diary entry on page 26 says, 'We sat down and ate
some chocolate.' How many different ways can you think
of to describe how they might have eaten the chocolate?

> We sat down and <u>eagerly</u> ate some
> chocolate.

2 Compare your list with a partner. Decide which adverb
you think fits best.

3 The writer talks about how he feels when he uses the
word 'hopefully'. Change these feeling words into adverbs.
They all end in -ly but you may need to check the
spelling in a dictionary.
anger – *angrily*
happy
sad
joyful
tearful
contented

4 Add any more 'feeling' adverbs you can think of, or find,
to your list.

Fact and opinion

If a reporter had spoken to the wife of Captain Cook or David Hempleman-Adams you might have read comments like this in the newspapers.

> Yesterday the traveller arrived home. His wife said, "He has been a long way. It is a great achievement."

Some of this is factual information – things that are accepted or can be proved to be true. It can be supported by evidence. Some of these **sentences** are opinions – what somebody thinks even though other people may disagree.

Fact

He has arrived home. (this can be seen by others)
He has been a long way. (this can be measured)

Opinion

It is a great achievement. (others might disagree)

1 Find two facts in the diary of David Hempleman-Adams and two facts in the passage about Captain Cook.

2 Find an opinion in each of the passages.

Facts | Opinions

3 List them.

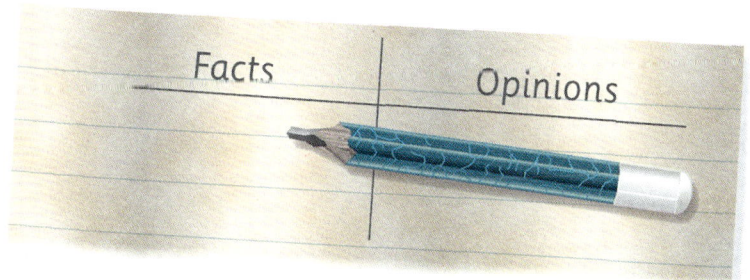

Opinions are sometimes signalled by certain words.

In my view…
I believe…
I think…
I feel…

4 Write a sentence about David Hempleman-Adams, beginning with one of these phrases.

5 Now read a current newspaper article. Underline two facts and two opinions.

Glossary
sentence

Writing a factual recount

You are going to write a first person factual recount based on a real event in your life.

TUESDAY, MAY 5, 1998

We've made it at last !

The concluding diary of David Hempleman-Adams who, with his companion Rune Gjeldnes, reached the North Pole on April 28

North Pole
Diary

Brainstorm

1 Think about a time when you went on a journey.

My journey to ...

Plan

2 Make notes under the following headings:

Key Facts

- When ?
- Where from ?
- Where to ?
- Who went ?
- Why going ?
- How ?

3 Now think of the order the events happened in and make a rough time line of what happened.

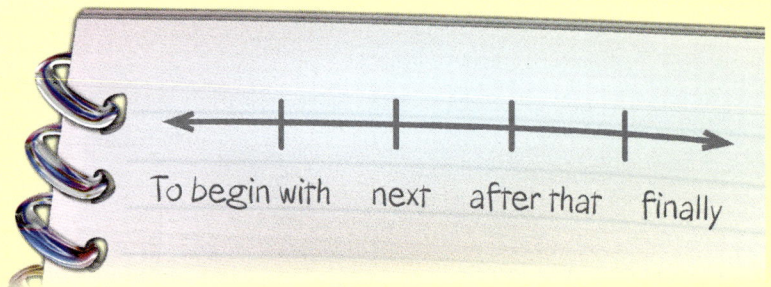

To begin with   next   after that   finally

4 Add details to your time line.
- How did it start (time, place) ?
- What happened then ?
- Next ?
- How did it end ?
- What was the final result ?
- What did you think and feel ?
- What was your opinion of the journey ?

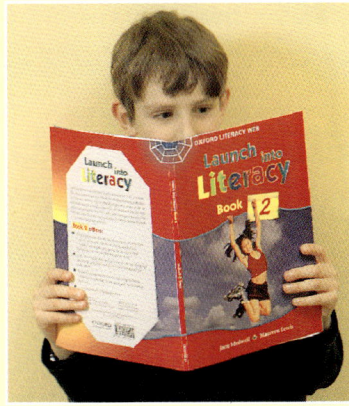

5 Reread the opening paragraph of the recount about Captain Cook on pages 18 and 19. Notice the key facts that are included.

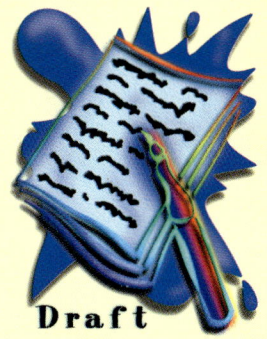

Draft

6 Reread the diary on page 26. Notice the personal pronouns and thoughts and feelings. Notice how the personal detail about the ripped trousers helps us get a sense of what it was like.

7 Now use your plans and the examples of writing you have reread to write a draft of your recount. Make sure the key facts and the chronological order are clear so that the reader will find your recount interesting and easy to follow. Put in personal thoughts and details.

Discuss

8 Swap your draft with a partner. Discuss these questions.
- Is it easy to understand?
- Are the important details in the opening?
- Is the order of events clear?
- Does the ending give us the outcome?
- Do we get a sense of the person writing this recount?

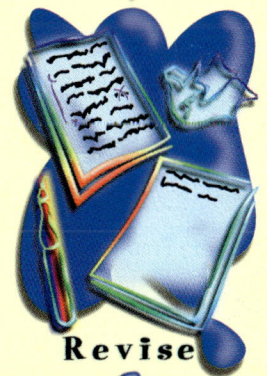

Revise

9 Talk about these questions with your partner and mark any changes you want to make on the draft. Check any spellings you are not sure about.

10 Write out your recount and then have a session when you read it aloud to your partner.

Publish

Writing to entertain

In this unit you are going to study science fiction and fantasy novels. You will consider the ways in which authors create other worlds and make them seem real and interesting.

Chapter 1

AN UNEXPECTED PARTY

the first sentence introduces the main character

In a hole in the ground there lived a hobbit. Not a nasty, dirty, wet hole, filled with the ends of worms and an oozy smell, nor yet a dry, bare, sandy hole with nothing in it to sit down on or to eat: it was a hobbit-hole, and that means comfort.

the setting is introduced at once

It had a perfectly round door like a porthole, painted green, with a shiny yellow brass knob in the exact middle. The door opened on to a tube-shaped hall like a tunnel: a very comfortable tunnel without smoke, with panelled walls, and floors tiled and carpeted, provided with polished chairs, and lots and lots of pegs for hats and coats – the hobbit was fond of visitors.

descriptive language

The tunnel wound on and on, going fairly but not quite straight into the side of the hill – The Hill, as all the people for many miles round called it – and many little round doors opened out of it, first on one side and then on another. No going upstairs for the hobbit: bedrooms, bathrooms, cellars, pantries (lots of these), wardrobes (he had whole rooms devoted to clothes), kitchens, dining-rooms, all were on the same floor, and indeed on the same passage. The best rooms were all on the left-hand side (going in), for these were the only ones to have windows, deep-set round windows looking over his garden, and meadows beyond, sloping down to the river.

location of the setting

details of the setting

This hobbit was a very well-to-do hobbit, and his name was Baggins. The Bagginses have lived in the neighbourhood of The Hill for time out of mind, and people considered them

the inhabitants of the setting

5

Look at this passage. It is the beginning of *The Hobbit*, a novel by J. R. R. Tolkien.

- How do you know this is the beginning of the novel?
- What makes you think that *The Hobbit* is a fantasy novel?
- Who lives in this setting?
- Look at the clue to the plot at the end of the passage. What do you think the story will be about?

very respectable, not only because most of them were rich, but also because they never had any adventures or did anything unexpected: you could tell what a Baggins would say on any question without the bother of asking him. This is a story of how a Baggins had an adventure, and found himself doing and saying things altogether unexpected. He may have lost the neighbours' respect, but he gained – well, you will see whether he gained anything in the end.

clue to the story

6

from *The Hobbit* by J. R. R. Tolkien

33

Comprehension

1 Reread the **extract** on pages 32 and 33.

2 Now answer these questions.

   a Hobbits live   underground?   in trees?   by rivers?

   b Most of the Bagginses were

       adventurous?   rich?   old?

   c List three ways in which the hobbit hole is made comfortable.

   d List three things which the hobbits enjoy.

   e What sort of story do you think this will be?
Write two sentences to say what it may be about.

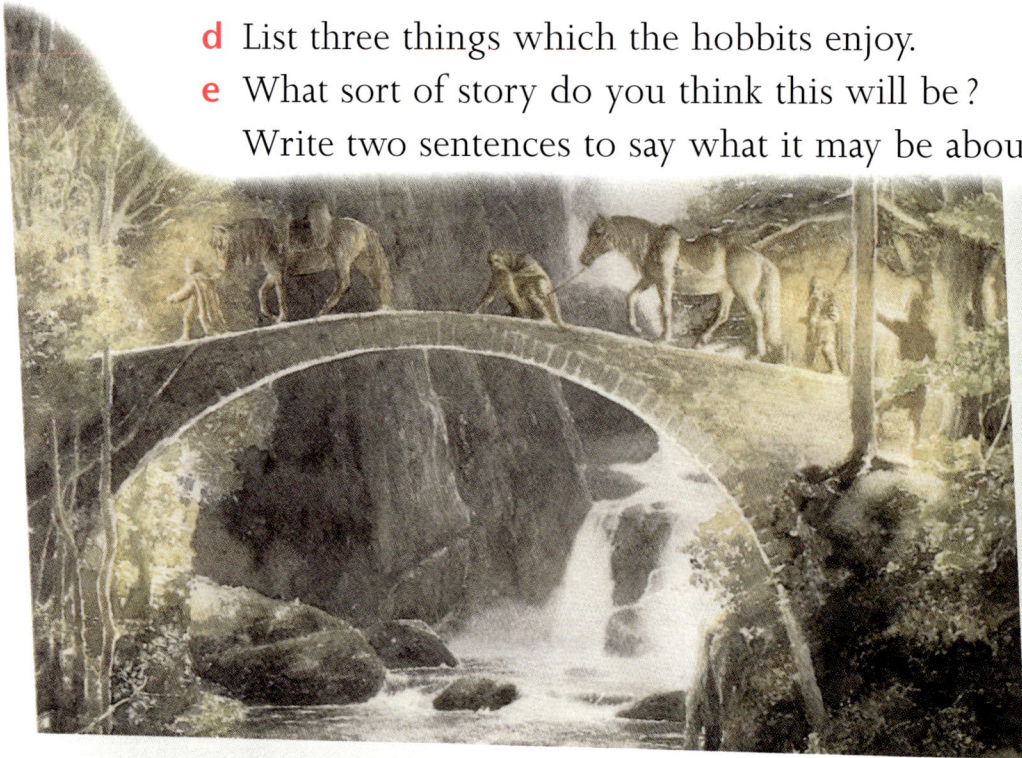

The **setting** of a story can tell us something about the **characters** in a setting.

3 Use the evidence in the passage to collect information about the character of the hobbit Baggins.

Evidence	Conclusion
• hobbit hole, and that means comfort	• likes to live comfortably
• shiny yellow brass door knob	• keeps things clean

Settings in detail

1 Reread the passage from *The Hobbit* on pages 32 and 33.

The hobbit hole is described in detail using **adjectives**.

EXAMPLE: It had a perfectly round door like a porthole, painted green, with a shiny yellow brass knob in the exact middle. The door

2 List the adjectives and **nouns** which are used to describe the hobbit hole in detail.

Adjectives	Nouns
perfectly round, green,	door
shiny, yellow	knob
tube-shaped	hall

3 Read another **extract** from *The Hobbit*, below.

The entrance to the path was like a sort of arch leading into a gloomy tunnel made by two great trees that leant together, too old and strangled with ivy and hung with lichen to bear more than a few blackened leaves. The path itself was narrow and wound in and out among the trunks. Soon the light at the gate was like a little bright hole far behind, and the quiet was so deep that their feet seemed to thump along while all the trees leaned over them and listened.

83

4 Select the words or phrases used to describe the following nouns.

   a the path   **b** the trees   **c** the quiet

5 Explain how the author makes the trees sound like evil beings.

Glossary
nouns
extract

35

Similes

Similes describe something by comparing it with something else.
EXAMPLE: It had a perfectly round, shiny door like a porthole.

1 Some similes use the word 'like'. Complete these similes.
   a The moon hung in the sky like ⬛⬛⬛ .
   b ⬛⬛⬛ like a herd of elephants.

2 Other similes use 'as ... as' to compare things. Complete these similes.
   a The night air was as cold as ⬛⬛⬛ .
   b The ⬛⬛⬛ was as black as soot.

When similes are used so often that they become boring we call them clichés.

3 Rewrite this passage, replacing the clichés with more interesting similes.

> The giant was as big as a house, with hair as black as night. His friend the troll was as old as the hills and they both looked as hungry as wolves. The big man had a face like thunder.

Old-fashioned words

Some words in a book can tell us about when it was written. Some of the words in *The Hobbit* are not used very much now, but might have been used by your grandparents. *The Hobbit* was written in 1937.

Glossary
definition

1 Look up these words in the dictionary and write a **definition** for each one.
   a pantry   b meadow   c frock   d parlour

Reading skills: *comprehension, comparing characters*

Settings and characters

Characters in a novel can tell us more about the **setting**

1 Read the **descriptions** of the hobbit and the faun. Fill in the chart below.

He was only a little taller than Lucy herself and he carried over his head an umbrella, white with snow. From the waist upwards he was like a man, but his legs were shaped like a goat's (the hair on them was glossy black) and instead of feet he had goat's hoofs. He had a red woollen muffler round his neck and his skin was rather reddish too. He had a strange, but pleasant little face, with a short pointed beard and curly hair, and out of the hair there stuck two horns, one on each side of his forehead. One of his hands, held the umbrella: in the other arm he carried several brown-paper parcels. What with the parcels and the snow it looked just as if he had been doing his Christmas shopping. He was a Faun. And when he saw Lucy he gave such a start of surprise that he dropped all his parcels.

77

from The Lion, the Witch and the Wardrobe by C. S. Lewis

I suppose hobbits need some description nowadays, since they have become rare and shy of the Big People, as they call us. They are (or were) a little people, about half our height, and smaller than the bearded dwarves. Hobbits have no beards. There is little or no magic about them, except the ordinary everyday sort which helps them to disappear quietly and quickly when large stupid folk like you and me come blundering along. They are inclined to be fat in the stomach; they dress in bright colours (chiefly green and yellow); wear no shoes, because their feet grow natural leathery soles and thick warm hair like the stuff on their heads (which is curly); have long clever brown fingers, good-natured faces, and laugh deep fruity laughs (especially after dinner, which they have twice a day when they can get it).

from The Hobbit

Characteristic	Hobbits	Fauns
Appearance	*half the height of humans*	
Clothes		
Character		*easily surprised/give presents*
Preferences	*like two dinners a day*	

2 The description of hobbits suggests that this story took place long ago. How do you know?

Glossary
setting
description

Comparing settings

You are now going to look more closely at a **setting** from a fantasy novel.

Here is an extract from *The Lion, the Witch and the Wardrobe*. This is a very famous fantasy novel in which a group of children help save a fantasy world.

> But at last he came to a part where it was more level and the valley opened out. And there, on the other side of the river, quite close to him, in the middle of a little plain between two hills, he saw what must be the White Witch's House. And the moon was shining brighter than ever. The House was really a small castle. It seemed to be all towers; little towers with long pointed spires on them, sharp as needles. They looked like huge dunce's caps or sorcerer's caps. And they shone in the moonlight and their long shadows looked strange on the snow. Edmund began to be afraid of the House.
>
> But it was too late to think of turning back now. He crossed the river on the ice and walked up to the House. There was nothing stirring; not the slightest sound anywhere. Even his own feet made no noise on the deep newly fallen snow. He walked on and on, past corner after corner of the House, and past turret after turret to find the door. He had to go right round to the far side before he found it. It was a huge arch but the great iron gates stood wide open.
>
> Edmund crept up to the arch and looked inside into the courtyard, and there he saw a sight that nearly made his heart stop beating. Just inside the gate, with the moonlight shining on it, stood an enormous lion crouched as if it were ready to spring. And Edmund stood in the shadow of the arch, afraid to go on and afraid to go back, with his knees knocking together. He stood there so long that his teeth would have been chattering with cold even if they had not been chattering with fear. How long this really lasted I don't know, but it seemed to Edmund to last for hours.

103

1 Answer these questions.
   a The main **character** in the extract is
      the White Witch?   Edmund?   the lion?
   b A turret is   *a window?   a tower?   a wall?*
   c How do you know that the extract takes place at night?
   d What is the weather like in the extract?
   e How does Edmund feel?

2 List five **adjectives** which describe the setting of this extract from *The Lion, the Witch and the Wardrobe*.

Glossary

setting
character
adjective

38

UNIT·3 **Writing to entertain**

Text features:
setting
Reading skills:
comprehension
Vocabulary:
gender words

3 Write two **similes** to describe the **setting** of this extract.

4 Compare the setting in *The Hobbit* (pages 32–33) with the setting in *The Lion, the Witch and the Wardrobe* (page 38). Fill in this chart.

Characteristic	The Hobbit	The Lion, the Witch and the Wardrobe
Place	A hobbit hole. Warm, clean, cosy, comfortable	
Time		Night. The moon is out.
Weather		
Characters	hobbits	

5 The atmosphere of the hobbit hole is warm and friendly. Write a sentence to describe the atmosphere of the setting in *The Lion, the Witch and the Wardrobe*.

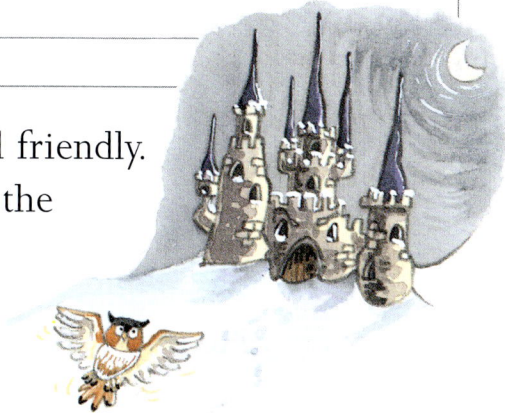

Gender words

Gender words tell you about the sex of the person or thing referred to. EXAMPLE: queen (**feminine gender**)
king (**masculine gender**)

1 Sort these words into two lists, feminine gender and masculine gender.

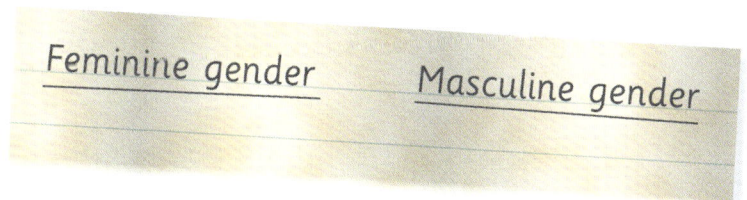

Feminine gender   Masculine gender

dog   girl   fox   lord   bitch   boy   lady   vixen

Some words have two forms, one for men and one for women. EXAMPLE: hero (masculine gender)
heroine (feminine gender)

Remember
The dictionary usually gives both forms of a word.

2 Copy and complete this chart.

Feminine gender	Masculine gender
prince	
	waitress
host	

Glossary
similes
setting
feminine gender
masculine gender

Comparatives and superlatives

Sometimes we use **adjectives** to compare one thing with another. These are called **comparative adjectives**.
EXAMPLE: The trees were **taller** than the bushes.
Superlative adjectives compare something with all the rest. EXAMPLE: He had the **biggest** feet in the class.

1 Write down the comparative and superlative forms of these adjectives. The first one is done for you.

Adjective	Comparative	Superlative
big	bigger	biggest
old		
new		
late		
small		

2 Complete these **sentences**.
  a My house is   than my auntie's house.
  b Tabitha is the   cat in the world.
  c Nanerl is   than Wolfgang.

To form the comparative you use the **suffix** -er. To form the superlative you use the suffix (ending) -est.
When an adjective ends in -y, the 'y' becomes an 'i'.
EXAMPLE: heav**y**   heav**i**er   heav**i**est
Sometimes the last letter of the adjective is doubled.
EXAMPLE: ma**d**   ma**dd**er   ma**dd**est

Remember
Use a dictionary to check your answers.

3 Make the comparative and superlative forms of these adjectives by changing the spelling and adding the correct suffix. tidy busy nosy silly thin fat big hot

If a word ends in -e, the 'e' is dropped before adding the suffix. EXAMPLE: larg**e**   larg**er**   larg**est**

Glossary
adjective
sentence

4 Write down the comparative and superlative forms of these words. wide brave wise safe

Irregular adjectives

Some **adjectives** have **irregular comparative** and **superlative** forms.
EXAMPLE: **good**, **better**, **best** not good, gooder, goodest
The best way to find out the comparative form of most adjectives is to look in the dictionary.

a b c d e f **g** h i j k l m n o

good *adjective* **better, best**
  1 what people like and praise. *a good story.*
  2 kind and true. *a good friend.*
  3 well behaved. *a good boy.*

goodbye *interjection*
  the word you say when you

gr

gr

1 Find the adjective 'bad' in the dictionary. Write down its comparative and superlative forms.

The comparative and superlative of longer adjectives are formed using **more** and **most**.
EXAMPLE: beautiful, **more** beautiful, **most** beautiful

2 Write down the comparative and superlative forms of these adjectives. **a** foolish **b** difficult **c** comfortable

Adjective	Comparative	Superlative
foolish	*more foolish*	*most foolish*
difficult		
comfortable		

3 Complete these **sentences**.
  a She is the ⬚⬚⬚ beautiful person I have ever seen.
  b The work was ⬚⬚⬚ difficult than Alex expected.

Glossary
sentence

Degrees of intensity

Some adjectives are about similar ideas but have different degrees of intensity.
EXAMPLE: degrees of heat – icy, cold, chilly, lukewarm, hot, burning

1 Arrange these groups of words in order of intensity.
  a ancient, newborn, young, old
  b hungry, famished, starving, peckish
  c thin, plump, fat, stout, obese

Science Fiction

Look at this picture from a science fiction **graphic novel**.

CAPTAIN'S LOG: STARDATE 41187.5

THE U.S.S. ENTERPRISE SLICES THROUGH THE PITCH THICKNESS OF AN UNMAPPED SECTOR LIKE A SHAFT.

PILOTED BY FEDERATION OFFICERS AND CREW, WHO ENGINEER EACH STEP OF OUR QUEST FOR UNDERSTANDING...

1 Look up 'science fiction' in your dictionary and write a **definition** using your own words.

2 The story in this picture is set in
   the present?   the past?   the future?

3 Who is on the spaceship?

4 A quest means   *a long search?   a trip?   getting lost?*

5 Here is a boring description of the Star Trek setting in the picture.

> The big, white spaceship flew along quickly like a seagull. Space was big, quiet, empty and black.

6 Choose interesting words to replace those underlined.
   EXAMPLE: big – vast, huge, massive, awesome, impressive

7 Now write a description of the setting which makes the reader imagine the atmosphere.

Remember

Science fiction lets us imagine the future.

Glossary

graphic novel
definition

Suspense and tension

UNIT·3 **Writing
to entertain**

Text features:
*suspense,
atmosphere*
Reading skills:
comprehension

In fantasy and science fiction stories authors use
suspense to make stories exciting. Suspense is the
uncertainty the reader feels when he or she does not
know what will happen.

1 Reread the passage on page 38. It ends with these words:
'... it seemed to Edmund to last for hours.'

2 What do you think might happen to Edmund?

3 Read this extract from *The War of the Worlds* by H. G. Wells.
In the book strange cylinders have landed on
Earth and no one knows what to expect.

A sudden chill came over me. There was a loud
shriek from a woman behind. I half turned, keeping
my eyes fixed upon the cylinder still, from which
other tentacles were now projecting, and began
pushing my way back from the edge of the pit.
I looked again at the cylinder, and ungovernable
terrors gripped me. I stood petrified and staring.

4 Write down what you think will happen next.

Writers use danger and mystery to create tension. In the
Animorphs series, Katherine Applegate describes how a group
of children try to stop aliens
from taking over the Earth.

My name if Rachel. I'm not going to tell you my
last name. I'm not going to tell you where I live.
I'll tell you all I can, because you need to know
what's going on. But I need to stay alive. If the
Yeerks knew who I was, I would be dead.
    But I will tell you the truth. Animorph. Animal
morpher. A human capable of becoming any
animal. It's our one weapon against the Yeerks, our
only power. Without it we're just five normal kids.

from *Animorphs 7: The Stranger*
by Katherine Applegate

4 Answer these questions.
a Why does Rachel keep
her full name and
address a secret?

b Do you think the Yeerks are
pets?   *aliens?*   *friends?*

c How can Rachel and her friends fight the Yeerks?

d Is this a good beginning to a story? Why?

Writing a novel

You are going to write a novel about a quest. On the journey your characters will encounter more than one setting. To help structure the novel you will need to write more than one chapter. You can write the novel on your own or with a friend.

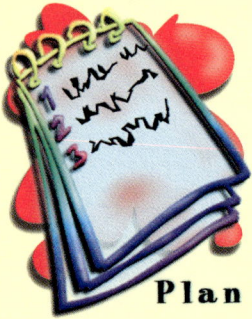

Plan

1 Decide whether your story is going to be a science-fiction story or a fantasy story.
Consider:
  • Will your story be set in the past, present or future?
  • Will your story be about this world or another world?

2 Choose a main character for your story.
You could choose:
  • a person (man, woman, child)
  • an alien or other type of fantasy being
  • an intelligent animal.

Draft

3 Write a detailed description of your character including:
  • their appearance
  • their personality
  • their feelings.
Use similes and adjectives.

4 In your novel your character will go on a quest. What they look for and where they go depends on what kind of character and world you have chosen for them.
  • A space journey might look for an important planet.
  • A fantasy story might look for a jewel, a crown or a princess.

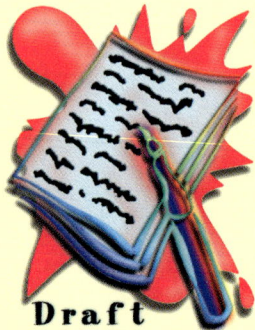

5 Use this planning grid to plan your novel in detail.

Chapter 1	When and where does the story begin ? Who is your character ? What is the character going to look for ?
Chapter 2	Your character begins the quest. Does your character go alone ? Where do they go first ?
Chapter 3	The quest continues. What problem arises ?
Chapter 4	Your character thinks of a way to solve the problem. The adventure happens. Ending.

6 Discuss this plan with a friend. Explain the plot of
the novel from your plan. When you have finished
ask your friend:
- Is the plot clear ?
- What do you think about the settings in the story ?
- Could I make it more exciting ?
- Is my character likeable ?

7 Write a draft of your novel. At the end of each chapter,
read it to your friend and ask for their advice.

8 Write out your novel.

Discuss

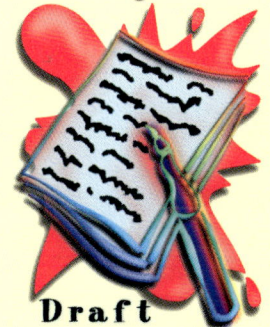
Draft

Publish

Writing to explain

In this unit you will study how explanations are written.
Explanations answer questions such as 'why?' or 'how?'.
At the end of the unit you will write
your own explanation.

a statement of answer

Transport Technology

a question

How do aeroplanes fly?

To fly, planes need to take off from the ground and then move forwards through the air. They use the force of air, their engines and their shape to help them do this.

details about what makes a plane fly

Take off
A plane can only take off if it moves quickly along the runway. Planes accelerate rapidly before take off. This makes the air push against the wings.

The wings are a special shape in order to make the air move over the top and bottom of the wings at different speeds.

How air moves over the aerofoil shape

Each wing is curved on top. This is called an aerofoil shape.

Air speeds up over the curved top

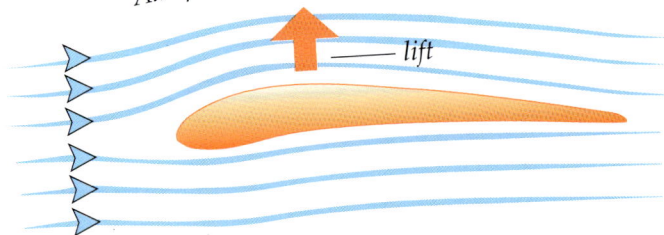

lift

16

- Why does this passage open with a simple statement of the answer?
- Why does this passage give details?
- Why does this passage include diagrams?
- Why are there technical words in the explanation?
- Why do explanations use words such as 'because' and 'this causes'?

further explanation in the diagram

Jet engines

The jet engine

aviation fuel burns in the combustion chamber and heats the air

spinning blades suck in the air

more details in the labels

jet of hot expelled air

Because speed is important, large aeroplanes have powerful jet engines. There are often two engines on each wing. A jet engine works by sucking in air. This air is heated by the fuel in the combustion chamber. This hot air then rushes out of the back of the engine. The force of this hot air pushes the plane forwards, along the runway or through the sky.

technical words

Controlling the plane

The pilot makes a plane go upwards by pulling a lever that controls the elevator flaps on the tail of the plane. To land he turns the elevators downwards. The part of the tail that sticks up into the sky is called the rudder. The rudder helps the plane turn smoothly. There are also flaps on the wings called ailerons which are used, with the rudder, to make the plane turn left or right.

present tense

17

from *Transport Technology* by Margaret Lawson

UNIT·4 **Writing to explain**

Reading skills:
comprehension,
Writing skills:
labelling
a diagram
Vocabulary:
word meaning,
using a dictionary

Understanding information

1 Reread the passage about air flight on pages 46 and 47.

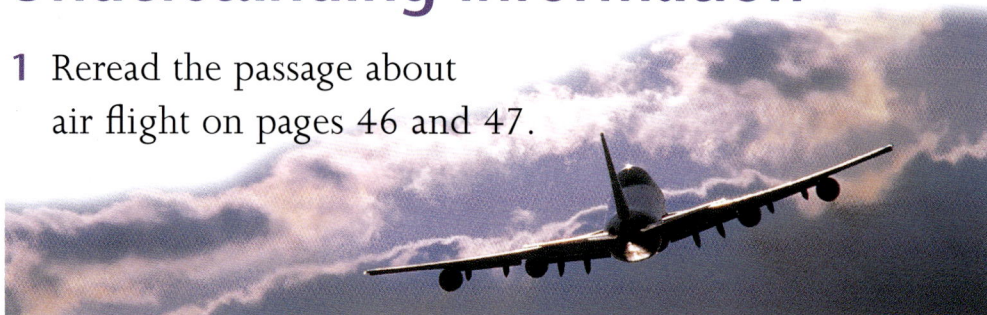

2 Now answer these questions.

a An aeroplane takes off when it is moving
quickly?   slowly?   smoothly?

b The top of an aeroplane wing is
curved?   flat?   triangular?

c Hot air causes the plane to
keep warm?   move forward?   stop?

d The ailerons are flaps on
the rudder?   the wings?   the engine?

e Jet engines use
petrol?   gas?   aviation fuel?

3 What do these words from the passage mean?
a aerofoil shape   **c** smoothly
b accelerate   **d** combustion

4 Check your answers in a dictionary.

5 Here is a diagram of a plane. Use the information in the passage on pages 46 and 47 to complete the labels a to e.

Parts of a plane that help it move

a
b
c   e
d

23

Joining sentences: cause and effect

Explanations often include a **description** of an action followed by the effect of that action.

EXAMPLE: The hot air rushes out of the engine.
The plane moves forward.

We could join these two **sentences** together with a **conjunction** that makes the link between the two events clear to the reader. These are called **causal conjunctions**.

EXAMPLE: The hot air rushes out of the engine **and as a result** the plane moves forward.
The plane moves forward **because** the hot air rushes out of the engine.

1 Here are some more causal conjunctions we might use to link actions and effects (results).

because **this caused**
so **consequently** **as**
this makes **as a result** **and so**

Remember
Your linking word can come at the beginning or in the middle of the sentence.

2 In the chart below are some actions and their effects. Use a causal conjunction to make each pair into one sentence.

Action	Effect
the flap on the wings move	the plane turns
a jet plane has powerful engines	it can accelerate quickly
air pushes against the wing of a plane	it takes off
I was naughty	my mum was cross
he washed the car	he was paid £1
I ate three bags of sweets	I felt sick

3 Finish these sentences by adding an effect to the action.

a I forgot my PE kit …

b The bus was late …

c The suitcase was very full …

d The alarm clock rang …

Glossary
description
sentence

49

Who does it belong to?

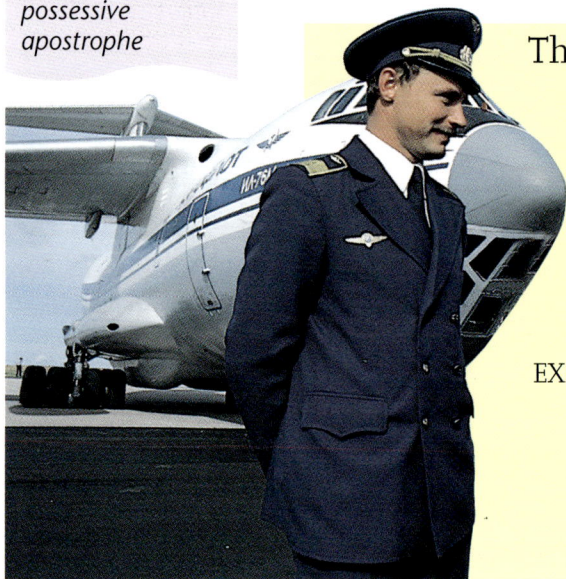

The pilot wears a hat. We could say, 'The hat of the pilot is navy blue,' but this sounds very clumsy. We usually say, 'The pilot's hat is navy blue.' The **'s** shows that the hat belongs to the pilot. This symbol **'** is called an **apostrophe**.

EXAMPLES: the crew of the aeroplane
– the aeroplane's crew
passengers of the airline
– the airline's passengers

1 Use an apostrophe and an s to show who the following things belong to. The first one has been done for you.
   a the coat of the girl – *the girl's coat*
   b the suitcase of the man –
   c the ticket of the boy –
   d the steps of the station –
   e the bark of the dog –
   f the bag of the woman –

2 There should be six apostrophes in this passage to show who things belong to. Write the passage out, putting the apostrophes in the correct places.

The boys ticket was missing. His mum searched in her handbag. She found her daughters passport, her sons passport and her own passport. She found her daughters ticket and her own ticket. Her sons ticket was not there. Dads face looked more and more angry. Suddenly her son shouted, 'Here it is!' and took it from his pocket.

How many does it belong to?

If a **noun** already has an s on the end of it because it is **plural** we just add the **apostrophe** symbol to show who things belong to. We don't add another s.

The boy's ticket (one boy)

The boys' tickets (more than one boy)

1 Do the following things belong to one person or thing or to more than one? Look where the apostrophe is and decide. Draw a picture to go with each phrase to show how many.
 a the girl's cake
 b the girls' cake
 c the cats' bowls
 d the train's wheels
 e the teacher's desk

a the girl's cake

Remember
We put the apostrophe after the existing **s** if it is a plural noun ending in **s**.

2 Put the missing apostrophes on this postcard. Decide whether the apostrophe goes before or after the s.

Dear Gran and Grandad,
The weather is good. The towns beach is great. The hotels food is super. Kids drinks are cheap. Sams ticket got lost on the journey but luckily he found it. We left Rover at the dogs kennels until we get back.
Miss you all.
Love from, Rita xxx

Mr & Mrs A. Mills
Manor Farm
High Ashton
Bicester
Oxon

Glossary
noun

51

Different forms of information

1 Look at this plane ticket and boarding pass.

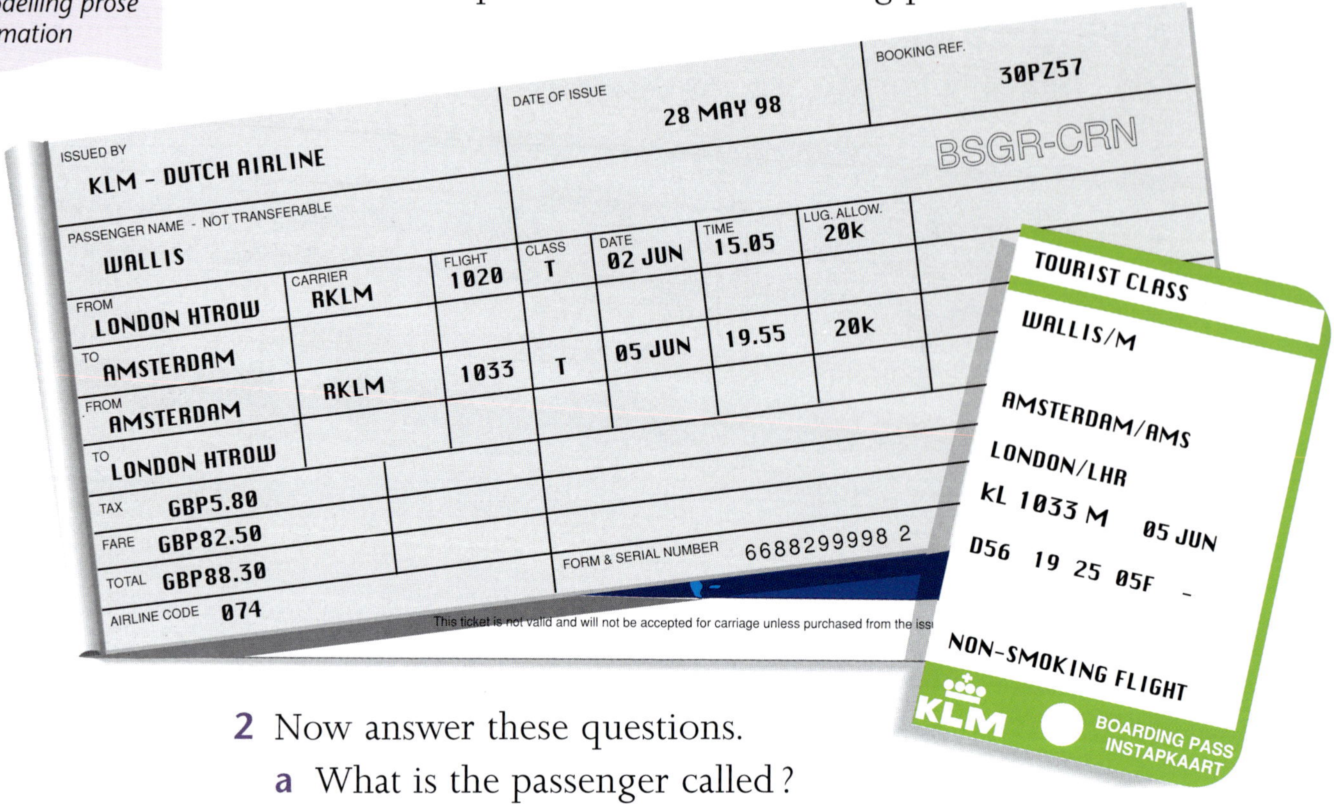

			DATE OF ISSUE	28 MAY 98		BOOKING REF.	30PZ57

ISSUED BY
KLM – DUTCH AIRLINE

BSGR-CRN

PASSENGER NAME - NOT TRANSFERABLE

		FLIGHT	CLASS	DATE	TIME	LUG. ALLOW.
WALLIS		1020	T	02 JUN	15.05	20k
FROM LONDON HTROW	CARRIER RKLM					
TO AMSTERDAM				05 JUN	19.55	20k
FROM AMSTERDAM	RKLM	1033	T			
TO LONDON HTROW						

TAX GBP5.80
FARE GBP82.50
TOTAL GBP88.30
AIRLINE CODE 074

FORM & SERIAL NUMBER 6688299998 2

This ticket is not valid and will not be accepted for carriage unless purchased from the issu

TOURIST CLASS

WALLIS/M

AMSTERDAM/AMS
LONDON/LHR
kL 1033 M   05 JUN
D56 19 25 05F

NON-SMOKING FLIGHT

KLM   BOARDING PASS
INSTAPKAART

2 Now answer these questions.

  a What is the passenger called?
  b Which cities is the plane flying between?
  c Which airport is the plane leaving from?
  d What time is the plane leaving London?
  e Which airline will the passenger be flying with?
  f Can you smoke on the flight?

3 Create your own airline ticket for this journey:

Sam Jones is travelling to Paris on 6 May. He is going to be there for two nights before flying back to London Gatwick. His outward bound Air France jet leaves at 13.10. His return home to England will mean an early start as the flight leaves at 06.30.

Never ch
onto an aircraft for s
Check-in staff will ask you questions ab
It is a criminal offence to give false information

This ticket is not valid and will not be accepted for carriage unless purchased from the issuing carrier or its authorized travel agent

Subject to conditions of contract in this ticket

Reasons why

These are some things you cannot take onto a plane.

WHAT AM I ALLOWED TO CARRY IN MY BAGGAGE ?

✗ **Firearms** of any type including replicas or toys;

✗ **Knives** or other implements with blades longer than three inches;

✗ **Explosives** – fireworks, flares, toy gun caps;

✗ **Gases** – camping or compressed gas cylinders, tear gas, CS gas devices;

✗ **Flammable materials** – petrol, lighter fuel, non-safety matches, fire lighters;

✗ **Poisons** – weed killers, insecticides;

✗ **Corrosives** – filled car batteries, mercury.

1 Think of the reasons why these things are banned and then complete this explanation.

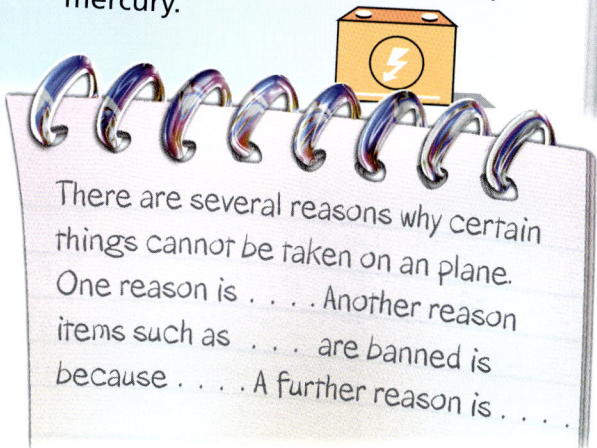

> There are several reasons why certain things cannot be taken on an plane. One reason is . . . . Another reason items such as . . . are banned is because . . . . A further reason is . . . .

Adding a reason to a **command** can turn it into a command and an **explanation** in one **sentence**.
EXAMPLE: Shut the door.
Shut the door so the cat does not get out.

2 Add reasons to these commands.
  a Be quiet.   **b** Hurry up.   **c** Listen carefully.

3 Think of two different reasons you might give to answer each of these questions.
  a Why are you late for school?
  b Why did the chicken cross the road?

Why are you late?

Because we overslept.

Because the Queen came for breakfast and I had to stay to meet her.

Glossary
command
sentence

53

How do ships sail?

Now we will look at another explanation and see how it is written.

a question

a statement of answer

details

technical word

Transport Technology

How do ships sail?

Ships sail on the sea because they float in the water and they have some form of power that pushes them through the water. Their shape also helps them to sail.

Floating in the water

Every object has a weight (gravity) that pushes it down. When a ship is in water gravity pushes it downwards. But the water pushes upwards (upthrust). If the force of the upthrust of deep water is stronger than the weight of the ship pushing downwards, the ship will float.

Travelling through water

Ships can be powered by wind (sails), by manpower (oars), or by engines. Big ships have steam turbine engines.

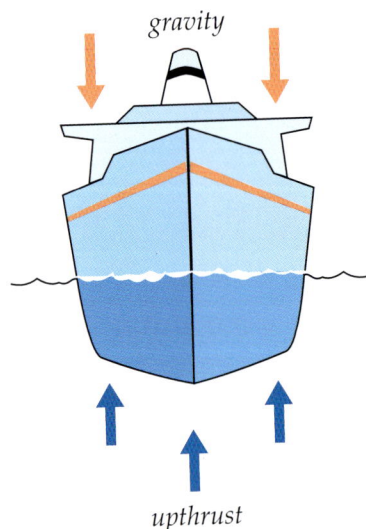

gravity

upthrust

1 Reread the passage and answer these questions.
   a What are the three factors that cause a ship to sail?
   b What are three ways of powering a ship?
   c What is the upward push of water called?
   d What is the pointed front of the hull called?
   e Why are the sides of the hull flat?

2 Find these words. What do you think they mean?
   a float means ...   c streamlined means ...
   b connected means ...   d rock means ...

Paragraphs

The passage is divided into four parts. Each part deals with one topic. Each chunk of writing is a **paragraph**. In non-fiction texts we sometimes also add headings to the paragraphs.

UNIT·4 **Writing to explain**

Text features:
paragraphs
Reading skills:
comprehension
Vocabulary:
word meanings

from *Transport Technology* by Margaret Lawson

Oil is used to heat water in a boiler. Steam from this enters the engine and makes the blades of the turbine spin. The turbine blades are connected to a propeller. The propeller turns and pushes the ship through the water.

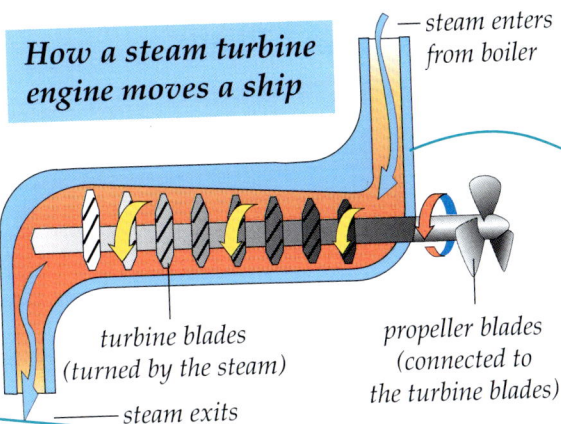

How a steam turbine engine moves a ship

steam enters from boiler

turbine blades (turned by the steam)

propeller blades (connected to the turbine blades)

steam exits

further explanation in the diagram

The shape of ships

The streamlined shape of a ship also helps it sail. The front of the ship's hull is pointed to push through the water. Its sides are flat so that the water flows smoothly along. The stern is rounded so that the water from the sides can meet again without making waves that would rock the ship.

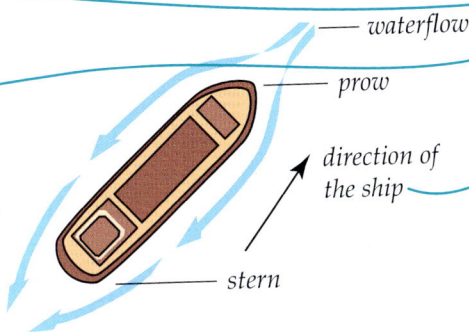

waterflow

prow

direction of the ship

stern

present tense

more details in the labels

1 This writing could be divided into three **paragraphs**.

The smallest types of boats are canoes and rowing boats. They can be for just one person and they are powered by human effort. Oars or paddles are used to push the boat through the water. Canoes and rowing boats have been used for thousands of years. However, once people discovered how to use the power of the wind to move the boat it was possible to build bigger boats. Some boats used just one sail but some of the large wooden ships had many sails and needed several masts to fly them from. Captain Cook used a sail-powered boat for his voyages of discovery. The largest ships of all use steam power to work their engines. Some modern ships such as tankers and cargo ships are enormous and need huge engines. Ships with engines do not depend on the wind and can move in any kind of weather.

- 21 -

2 Complete these **sentences**.

   a I would start the first paragraph with the words …

   b I would start the second paragraph with the words …

   c I would start the third paragraph with the words …

Glossary
sentence

55

Adding endings to words

The explanation on page 54 includes the **sentence**, 'Ships can be powered by ...'. 'Powered' is the **verb** in this sentence. The word 'powered' is made from the root noun 'power' + the ending -ed. If we add a different ending to 'power' we change it into an adjective.

EXAMPLE: power + ful = powerful

He was a powerful singer.

The bit we add to the end of a word like this is called a **suffix**.

1 Look at how this word changes by adding a suffix.

noun	adjective	verb
boast	boast**ful**	boast**ed**

2 Change these words in the same way by adding suffixes.

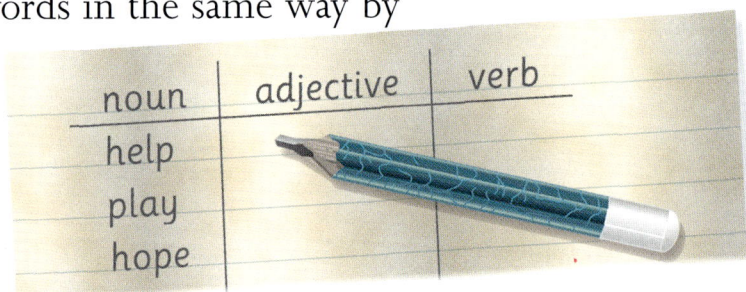

noun	adjective	verb
help		
play		
hope		

3 Now use each word in a sentence to show its different function in the sentence.

One example has been done for you.

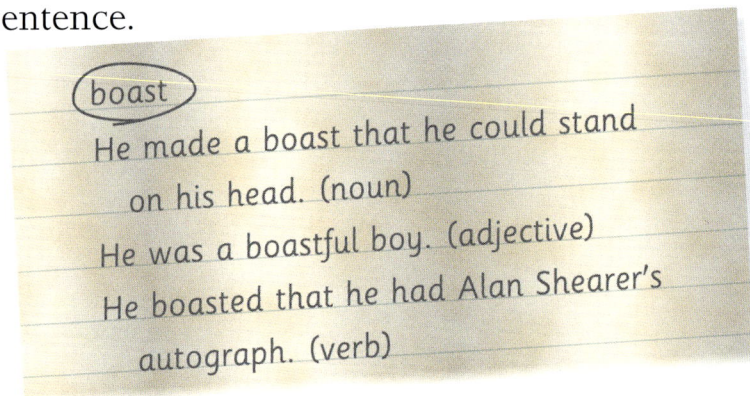

> boast
>
> He made a boast that he could stand on his head. (noun)
> He was a boastful boy. (adjective)
> He boasted that he had Alan Shearer's autograph. (verb)

4 Add the correct suffix so that these sentences make sense.
   a She rode a power____ motorbike.
   b The movement of the boat rock____ the baby to sleep.
   c He sail____ from Liverpool to New York.
   d The plane was peace____ as the passengers slept.

Adding more endings to words

The explanation on page 55 says 'the water flows smoothly'. 'Smoothly' is an **adverb**. It has been made by adding the **suffix** -ly to the root word 'smooth'.

a b c d e f g h i j k l m n o p q r **s** t u v w

smooth *adjective* **smoother, smoothest**
1 without any lumps or rough parts. *a smooth surface.*
2 without any bumps or jerks. *a smooth ride.*
smoothly *adverb*

snare *noun* **snares**
a trap for catching an

snarl *verb* **snarls, snarling,**
to make the sound a dog
when it is angry.

1 Make new words by adding the suffix -ful or -ly. Say whether the new word is an **adjective** or an adverb.

   beauty   cross   sad   proud   truth   thank

   You may need to check the spelling of your new word in a dictionary.

2 Can you add both suffixes together to any of the words? If you think you can, write down the new words that you create.

3 Reread the 'How do ships sail?' passage. Look for examples of these common suffixes.

watering   smoothly   -ess   -er   -ful   -al   -es   -able   -est   -ly   -ing

4 Find ten words in the passage which are a root word plus a suffix. Make a list of the word, its root and its suffix.

word	root	suffix
floating	float	ing

Glossary
adverb
adjective

57

Writing an explanation

You are going to write an explanation about how a skateboard moves.

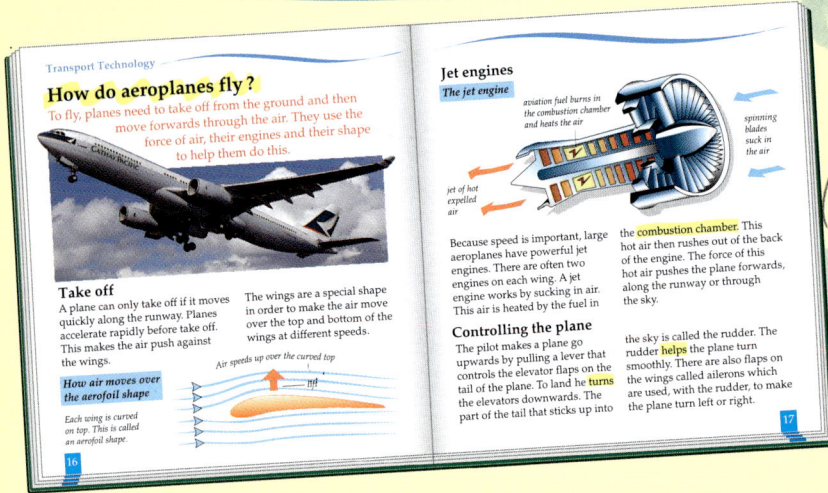

Brainstorm

Plan

1 Reread the explanations about how a plane flies on page 46 and how a ship sails on page 54. Notice that these explain:
- what powers the movement
- how their shape helps them to move
- what forces are involved.

2 Write rough notes on planes, ships and skateboards using the explanations in this book, any knowledge of your own and anything you have read. Your teacher will also give you an information sheet on skateboards to read.

Comparing different ways of travelling
Unit 4 PCM 32

Write rough notes on planes, ship and skateboards. Use the chart to help you.

	Planes	Ships	Skateboards
Powered by		wind humans fuel	humans
Shape			
Forces			
Any other details			

Unit 4 PCM 31

Skateboards were invented in the 1960s. Surfers in California wanted to try 'surfing' on dry land. They put a surfboard shaped piece of wood on wheels. Since then lighter and more manoeuvrable skateboards have been developed.

The basic skills a rider needs to use a skateboard are balance and board control. The skateboard is moved by pushing it along. The rider puts one foot on the board and uses the other foot to push the board along. Once the board is moving the pushing foot is put on the board.

To control the board you have to be able to turn it. To turn a board you lean in the direction of the turn. If you lean back on your heels it turns in that direction. Leaning towards the toes turns the board the other way. This is called 'carving'.

Once skateboarders can move forward and carve they can start doing more complicated moves such as ollies, grabs and flips. A grab is when you hold the board with one hand in the middle of a jump. There are lots of different grabs depending on which hand is used and which part of the board is grabbed. There are also lots of different flip tricks. In a flip the board is flipped over when the skater is in the air.

Skateboarders use other words to describe their actions. They say they are moving 'frontside' or 'backside'. Frontside means they are facing the ramp when they make a jump. Backside means they are facing away from the ramp as they make a jump.

Skateboarding can be done in the streets or on special ramps. The smoother the surface the faster the skateboard can travel. The height and steepness of the ramp also makes a difference to the speed. The steepest, fastest ramps are called vert ramps. Adjusting the king pin also affects the speed of the board.

Skating can be dangerous so safety is important. Skaters need to know how to fall. They also need to wear hard pads and a helmet to protect themselves.

3 Read the opening question and write a brief reply using your notes. This is your opening:

How do skateboards move?

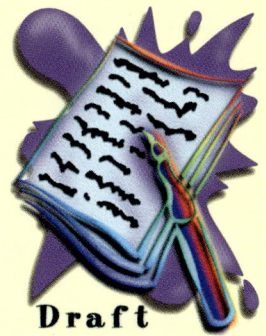

Draft

4 Now go through each of the factors you have mentioned in your opening and add more detail. You can:
- include diagrams
- make each part of the explanation a separate paragraph
- add headings to your paragraphs if you wish
- use causal conjunctions to link cause and effect sentences.

5 Think about how you are going to lay out your explanation.
- Where will any diagrams go?
- Do you need pictures?
- What size print should the sub-headings be?

Revise

6 Swap your draft with a friend. Discuss these questions.
- Is it easy to understand?
- Are the important factors summarized in the opening?
- Do the diagrams help?

7 Talk about these questions with your partner and mark any changes you want to make on the draft. Check any spellings you are not sure about.

8 Complete your final version and have a session reading it aloud to your partner.

Publish

Writing to persuade

In this unit you will look at how we can use language to persuade people. At the end of the unit you will produce your own poster or leaflet to persuade people to follow the rules of your classroom.

big print is easy to read from far away

headings for each paragraph

each paragraph makes a new point

Being Sun

Safe in the sun
It is very important to look after your skin. Young skin is very delicate and damage can sometimes be permanent and cause serious problems later in life. By following simple guidelines you can still enjoy the sunshine.

You don't need a tan
You look and feel just as good with an untanned skin. Don't hurt your skin. Protect your skin against the sun and the problems it may cause you in the future.

Avoid the midday sun
UV light is strongest in the summer between 11 am and 3 pm. Avoid staying out in the sun in the middle of the day.

Spend time in the shade
You can play in the shade, under trees or beach umbrellas, to avoid getting sunburned.

LABORATOIRES
GARNIER
AMBRE
SOLAIRE

Be sun smart

Look at how this poster works.

- How does the poster get your attention?
- What important points does the poster make?
- Who might have written this poster?
- Who is this poster written for?
- What does the poster persuade you to do?

Smart

When the sun is up COVER UP!

the illustrations make you look at the poster

Cover up
In the hot sun, wear a wide brimmed sun-hat to protect your head and neck. Cool, loose clothes will protect your arms and legs.

Always use a sunscreen
Choose the sun protection factor (SPF) for your skin type, and rub in the sunscreen carefully on all the skin which is exposed to the sun. Skin doctors (dermatologists) recommend that children should always use a high protection factor, at least SPF 15. Re-apply your sunscreen generously at regular intervals, especially after playing in water.

main point of the paragraph

Drink plenty
When you are hot, you sweat and lose water. Drink water to replace it so you don't get dehydrated (too dry).

more information

61

UNIT·5 Writing to persuade

Reading skills:
comprehension
Grammar,
Punctuation:
*contractions,
apostrophes*

Understanding the passage

1 Reread the poster on page 60 and 61 and answer these questions.

 a Why should you avoid the sun?

 b When is the safest time to go out in the sun?

 c Where can you find shade?

 d At what time of year would you expect to see a poster like this and why?

2 Answer these questions about words from the passage. Check your answers in a dictionary.

 a 'Delicate' means   tough?   needing care?   white?

 b 'Permanent' means

  lasts forever?   goes away quickly?   very serious?

 c 'Sunscreen' means

  cream to put on your skin in the sun?

  an umbrella?   a television programme?

 d A 'dermatologist' is

  a sunny place?   a skin doctor?   a plant?

3 Write a sentence that gives the poster's main message.

4 How do you know that this poster is aimed at children?

Contractions

In the poster, '**Do not** hurt your skin' is written as '**Don't** hurt your skin'. A shortened word like this is called a **contraction**. We shorten words by using an **apostrophe** (') to show where letters are missing.

EXAMPLES: do not = don't
   they are = they're
   I have = I've
   can not = can't

1 Write out the full forms of these contractions.

aren't we're won't you're can't I'm haven't she's

Grammar, Punctuation: *contractions, apostrophes*
Text features: *formal and informal language*

There are two main types of **contraction**.
One type is a **verb** + 'not'.
EXAMPLE: have + not = haven't
Another type of contraction includes a **pronoun** + a verb.
EXAMPLE: I + have = I've

2 Make as many contractions as you can using the verbs listed below + 'not'. The first is done for you.

can + not =
will + not =
have + not =
were + not =
are + not =
is + not =

can + not = can't

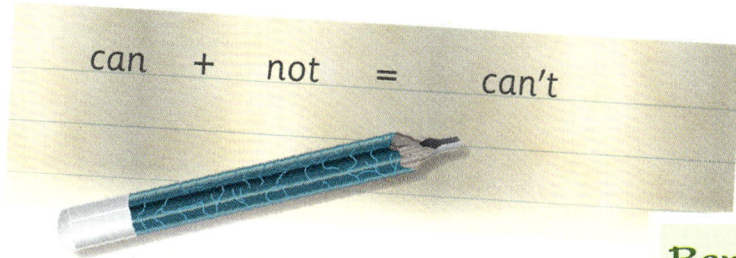

Remember
Not is negative.

3 Make as many contractions as you can using these pronouns and verbs.
EXAMPLE: I + will = I'll

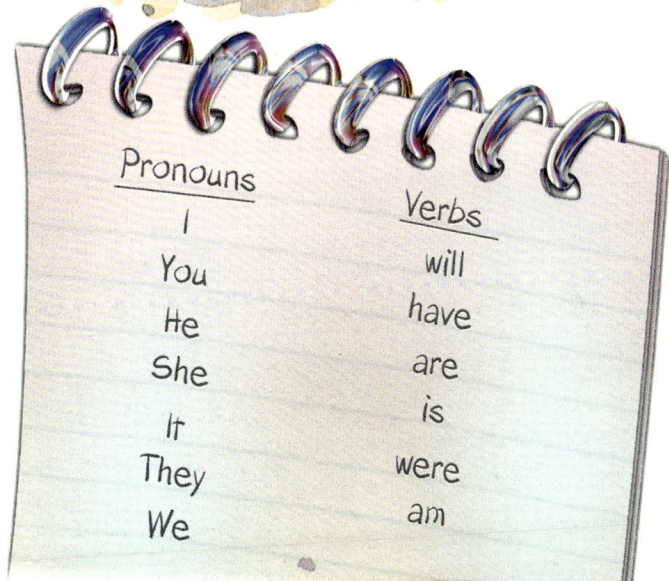

Pronouns	Verbs
I	
You	will
He	have
She	are
	is
It	
They	were
We	am

4 Rewrite these sentences and change the contractions into their full form.
  a It's time for break.
  b You can't stay out in the sun for too long.
  c We're going on a trip tomorrow.
  d Don't run in the corridor.
  e It won't be long until playtime.

Remember
It's always means **it is**.

Glossary
verb
pronoun

63

Formal and informal language

Posters, adverts and letters are often written in **informal language**. Informal language sounds friendly or like speech. Informal language includes **contractions** and informal words.

1 Here is a note. Rewrite it using contractions.

> When you come to stay do not be late or else we will not be able to go swimming. Do not worry if you have not got a costume. I am the same size as you so you can borrow one of mine. We will go to the beach. Do not forget your sunscreen then you need not worry about getting burnt.

2 Read both versions of the note aloud to a friend.
- Does one version sound more like talk?
- Which version sounds informal (relaxed, friendly)?
- Which sounds more formal?

3 Read these two letters.

> Dear Mrs Jones
> I'm writing to tell you that at around ten today I was driving along Baker Street, near your house, when I had to swerve to avoid a cat. Unfortunately I hit your gate ...

> Dear Madam,
> I am writing to inform you that at approximately 10 a.m. this morning I was proceeding along Baker Street in the vicinity of your dwelling, when I was obliged to manoeuvre to avoid a cat. Unfortunately I collided with your gate ...

4 Make a list of the words and phrases which are different in the formal and informal letter.

Formal words and phrases	Informal words and phrases
Madam	Mrs Jones
I am	I'm

Questions and commands

UNIT·5 **Writing to persuade**

Grammar:
imperative verbs
Punctuation:
*question marks
and full stops*

Letters, **advertisements**, posters and other writing which persuades often contains **questions** and **commands**.

gets your attention

Do you want to protect your skin?
Use **SuperSUN** sunscreen.
SuperSUN sunscreen stops you from burning.

tells you what to do

Do you want silky skin?
Use **SuperSUN** sunscreen.
SuperSUN keeps your skin super soft.

Super Sun for a super skin!

1 Write out the two questions in this advertisement.

2 Write out the command in this advertisement.

3 The **sentences** below are questions. Change them into commands by removing words and **question marks**. The first one is done for you.

> ~~Do you~~ Go to bed early every night ~~?~~.
> Go to bed early every night.

  a Do you go to bed early every night?
  b How often do you walk to school?
  c When do you do some exercise?

4 These sentences are commands. Make them into questions by adding words and question marks.

> Eat an apple every day.
> Do you eat an apple every day?

  a Eat an apple every day.
  b Brush your teeth at night.
  c Wear a hat in the sun.

Remember
Use a capital letter to start each sentence.

Glossary
advertisement
question
command
sentence

Reading an advertisement

Here is a poster which aims to persuade schools to buy caps for their children. **Advertisements** like this contain a lot of information.

Safe fun in the sun

The baseball cap

The legionnaires cap

Popular amoungst older children

Specially designed to protect children's necks from the sun

Plastic adjuster — one size fits all children

Elasticated insert means one size fits all children

Ventilation eyelets

Ventilation eyelets

100% washable cotton

100% washable cotton

Order form

COSTS	1–99	100–199	200 +	Red	Navy	White	Blue	Green	Yellow	Total cost
Legionnaires caps	£2.50	£2.25	£2.00							
Baseball caps	£1.90	£1.80	£1.70							£ 5.00

I have enclosed my cheque ☐   Contact name:

Contact tel no: Delivery address:

Carriage

Total cost

Total amount payable

1 Read it carefully. Now answer these questions.
   a In what colours are the hats made?
   b What different styles of caps are offered for sale?
   c What will happen if you order more than 200 caps?
   d What does the slogan claim that the caps will do?
   e Which hat would you chose and why?

2 Design a sunhat, with a **logo** on it, for your school.

Glossary
advertisement
logo

Slogans and headlines

A good headline or **slogan** tells you the main message of a poster or article and makes it easy to remember.

EXAMPLE: 'Slip Slap Slop' helps us to remember to slip on a shirt, slap on a hat and slop on some sunscreen.

HAT → SHIRT → SUNSCREEN

SLIP! SLAP! SLOP!

1 Go back to the posters and **advertisements** in this unit. Write down their slogans and say what they mean.

Here are a few more slogans.

Hot tip - don't fry

Move into the shade

Play safe in the Sun

2 Make a list of slogans you have seen recently. Write down what message each one is trying to give.

Slogans often use words that:

- rhyme EXAMPLE: Street Heat
- have two meanings EXAMPLE: Stay Cool
- repeat the same letters and/or sounds EXAMPLE: Beat the Burn.

Street Heat

Stay Cool

Beat the Burn

3 Copy the chart and add your slogans to the columns. You may want to add other columns.

Rhyming slogans	Slogans with two meanings	Slogans which repeat a sound
Street Heat	Stay Cool	Beat the Burn

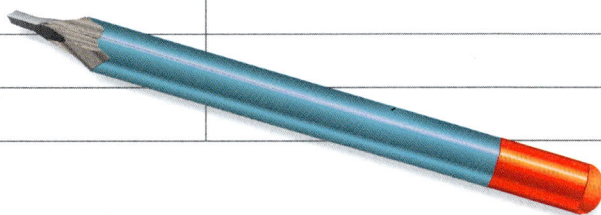

Glossary
slogan
advertisement

Points of view

1 Read this newspaper article.

The school cap is back

Caps have been introduced at Oaklands School in Crowthorne, Berkshire. Gone is the little woollen cap... in its place is a cap with flaps to protect young skin against Britain's increasingly hot summers. "It's to protect against the sun," said Anthony Griffiths, 8. "The flap at the back protects your neck and the front protects your eyes." David Beazer, 11, says it's "cool" to be able to wear baseball caps at school. Jean Fice, the school secretary explains, "Our motto here is: 'The sun has got his hat on' and so should our pupils."

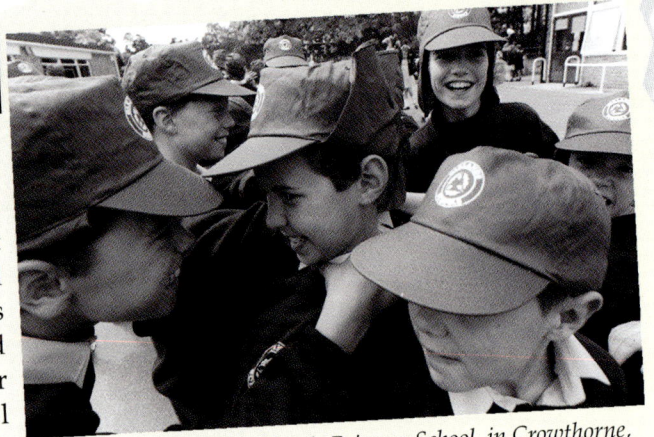

New caps on show at Oaklands Primary School, in Crowthorne, Berkshire, one of 50 schools where headgear is back.

2 Discuss the article and answer these questions.
   a What is the main message of this newspaper report?
   b What reasons for children to wear caps are given in the article?
   c How do the children feel about wearing caps?
   d Why did the newspaper report this story?

They will get lost.

They cost too much.

They'll look cool.

They'll save their skin.

3 Make a list like this one, giving as many reasons as you can think of for and against having caps.

Reasons for	Reasons against
They shade your eyes.	They make your head sweat.

Joining ideas

When you write to persuade someone you need to join your ideas together. Words which link ideas together are called **connectives**

and   because   also   but

1 Write down the connectives which fit into the spaces in these **sentences**

   a Sara uses sunscreen ▢ she doesn't want to get burnt.
   b Jamil likes the sun ▢ he doesn't want to burn.
   c Mum loves summer ▢ likes to sunbathe.

2 Some connectives start a new sentence.

   However   On the other hand   Even so

   a Fresh air is good for you. ▢ you can get sunburn outside.

   b It is important to stay in the shade, to drink water and to use a hat. ▢ you should avoid the midday sun.

3 Read this **draft** letter written to parents.

Duck Green School

```
Dear Parents,

Welcome back to the summer term. It is great to see everyone.
____ we must tell you all about an important issue.
     The sun is very hot ____ it can be dangerous. You should
ask your children to wear hats in the playground ____ they
will protect the children's heads.
     We know that the sunshine makes everyone feel good. ____
it can also cause very serious sunburn. This looks ugly ____
it is dangerous. It makes children sick and dizzy. ____ it can
damage their skin forever.

Yours sincerely
```

4 The ideas in this letter need to be joined up. Rewrite the letter putting in the missing connectives.

Writing a letter to persuade

Todd told Miss Smith that he didn't enjoy playtime. This is what he said.

> There's no space to talk. I wanted to talk to Jeannie and the football hit me on the head. I've got a bruise on my forehead. It was an accident but it's not the first time it's happened. It's happened to other children too. There isn't enough space to talk because people play football everywhere. Why can't they play at one end so we can do other things at the other end?

1 Answer these questions.
  a What is the problem in the playground?
  b What solution does Todd suggest?
  c Who should he try to persuade to change things?

Todd and Jeannie did a survey about behaviour in the playground. This is what they found.

Playground problems

Want a football-free area	JHT JHT JHT \\\\\
Want football throughout the playground	JHT /|||

2 Complete the **draft** of a letter to Todd's headteacher.

Dear Mrs Highlie,

I am writing to you about the problem of accidents in the playground caused by footballs ...ing

The problem is that .....

The children in our class think .....

I would like you to .....

Yours sincerely

Glossary
draft

70

Listing and bullet points

Instead of **commas** in sentences, information books and leaflets often use **bullet points** to draw attention to important details. A bullet point looks like a fat full stop at the beginning of a line.

We can use bullet points if we want to make something stand out.

EXAMPLE: You should not be noisy in class by shouting, singing, talking while the teacher is talking or banging pens and pencils.

BECOMES You should not be noisy in class by
  • shouting
  • singing
  • talking while the teacher is talking
  • banging pens and pencils.

1 A school has written an information sheet about a school trip. Redesign the sheet and use bullet points to make the **lists** look more eye-catching.

School trip
The following items are needed during your child's visit to the school camp. Jeans or long trousers, a sweater, sweatshirt, walking shoes, indoor shoes or slippers, towels, socks, underwear and night clothes are required. Each child needs a wash bag containing a toothbrush, toothpaste, soap, a flannel, shampoo, hairbrush or comb. Shorts, T-shirts, a swimming costume, towel, a sunhat and suncream will also be needed for fine weather.

Bullet points can also be used to emphasize the main points of a piece of writing.

2 Reread what Todd said to his teacher on page 70. Complete the bullet points below.

Todd's main points were:
  • a football had hit his head
  • footballs in the playground are dangerous
  •
  •

Glossary
comma
list

Writing a poster

In this unit you have looked at how we can write to persuade people. Now design a poster to persuade children to follow the rules of your class.

When Mrs Smith asked her class what the class rules were she got all sorts of answers.

Listen to other people when they speak. Don't speak when they're speaking. That way we can understand each other and listen.

Be sensible because otherwise the others can't work.

No pushing.

Don't make too much noise, like shouting or laughing, so that people can work.

Plan

Planning – You need to plan your poster to make sure you put in the right information.

1 Make a list of all the rules you think are important in your class.

2 Look at your ideas. Write down the main points and the reasons for them in a chart.

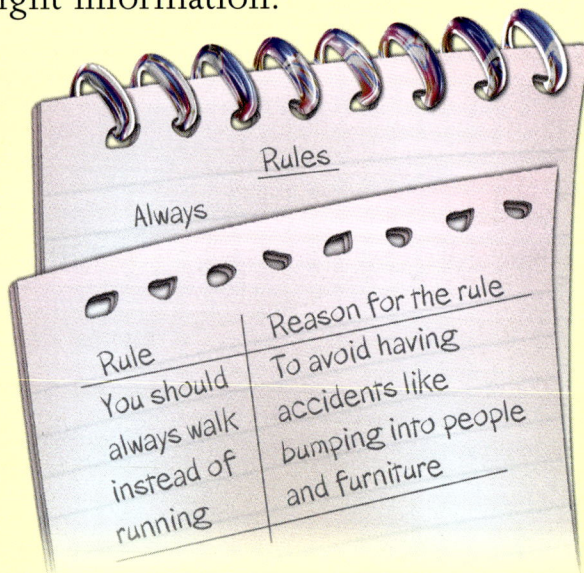

Rules

Always

Rule	Reason for the rule
You should always walk instead of running	To avoid having accidents like bumping into people and furniture

Drafting – You write a first draft so that you can see how your poster might be written.

3 Using the rules chart you filled in above, write a draft of a poster which tells other children what the class rules are and why they should follow them.

4 Invent a slogan for your poster. It should help the reader to remember the point of your poster.

Draft

Revising – You should revise your draft to make sure your poster says what you want it to, in a clear way. You can make changes at this point.

5 Check you have used commands to make the rules clear. Check that you have given reasons for your rules.

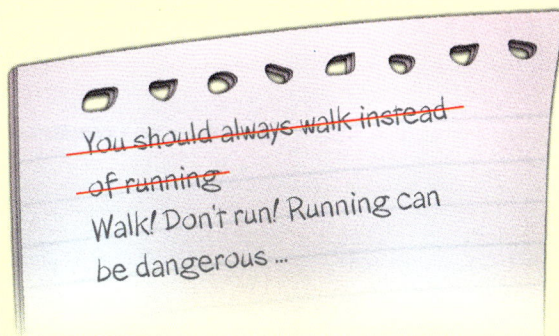

6 Discuss your draft with another person.
   a What is the main point? Is it clear?
   b Does the poster give good reasons to follow the rules?
   c Will readers understand what the slogan means?

7 Mark any changes you want to make on your draft.

Editing – You should edit your work to make sure that your poster is well written.

8 Mark any spelling, full stop, comma or capital letter changes on your draft in another colour.

Designing layout – You design the layout so that the poster will look as interesting as possible. This is when you put in the pictures and illustrations.

9 Choose some pictures or draw illustrations for your poster. Remember, illustrations grab the reader's attention.

10 Use a sheet of paper to plan the way you will set out your poster. You may need to move the words, slogan and pictures around.

Publishing

11 When you have made a final draft of your poster put it up where others can see it.

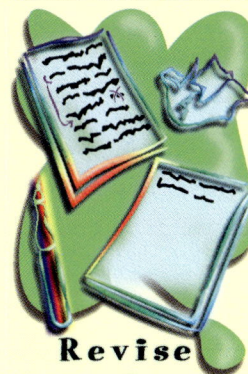
Revise

Edit

Design

Publish

Glossary

account   A piece of speech or writing which tells us about an event.

adjective, comparative, superlative   A word that goes with a noun and tells us about it. EXAMPLE: a blue balloon. A comparative adjective can be used to compare nouns. EXAMPLE: The boy was bigger than his friend. A superlative adjective can be used to compare something with all the others. EXAMPLE: The boy was the biggest in the class.

adverb   A word that tells us about a verb. Some adverbs have the suffix ly. EXAMPLES: happily, merrily

advertisement   An advertisement tells us about things which are for sale or which are going to happen.

alliteration   A number of words close together which begin with a similar consonant sound. EXAMPLES: ten tired teddies, sliding slithery snakes

apostrophe   An apostrophe is a mark used to show that a letter has been left out. EXAMPLE: he is can be written as he's Apostrophes are also used to show ownership. EXAMPLES: the cat's bowl (1 cat), the cats' bowls (more than 1 cat)

argument   A written argument makes a point and gives evidence to support it.

brainstorm   A way of writing down ideas when planning writing. Words are arranged around the topic you are thinking about.

bullet point   A bullet point is a punctuation mark used to emphasize items in a list. EXAMPLE: • sugar   • milk

category word   A category word describes a set of items. EXAMPLE: the category word footwear includes shoes, slippers, socks etc.

character   A character is an individual in a story, play or poem. The things they do and say tell us what they are like.

chronological order/non-chronological   Chronological order is the order in which events happen. Chronological writing is written in time order. EXAMPLE: an account of a day that starts in the morning and goes through to the evening. Non-chronological writing is not written in time order.

clause   A distinct part of a sentence including a verb. A main clause makes sense on its own. A subordinate clause adds detail to the main clause but does not make sense on its own. EXAMPLE: Although it was foggy, I went out.
        (subordinate clause) (main clause)

comma	A punctuation mark used to break up sentences so that they are easier to understand. Commas are used to separate items in a list that is part of a sentence. EXAMPLE: I bought eggs**,** fish and some chocolate.
command	A sentence telling someone to do something. One of four sentence types (exclamation, question and statement are the others).
compound word	A word made from two other words. EXAMPLE: footpath
conjunction	A conjunction is a word used to join sentences or parts of sentences. EXAMPLES: and, but, then, because
connective	A word or group of words which links sentences or parts of sentences. EXAMPLES: and, then, but, even, so
consonant/ vowel	In the English alphabet there are 5 vowels (a e i o u) and 21 consonants (b c d f g h j k l m n p q r s t v w x y z).
contraction	Words which are shortened by replacing one or more letters with an apostrophe. EXAMPLE: do not = don't
definition	A statement giving the meaning of a word or phrase.
description	Words which enable the reader/listener to form an idea of an object, event or feeling.
dictionary entry	Information given about a word in a dictionary.
draft	A piece of writing which is not in finished form. A final draft is a piece of writing that is finished.
edit	To change the grammar, spelling, punctuation or words in writing before it is finished.
exclamation	A type of sentence that expresses strong feeling. Exclamations end with an exclamation mark. EXAMPLE: Help me, please **!** One of four sentence types (question, statement and command are the others).
extract	A piece of text taken out of the longer text.
fiction/non-fiction	Fiction is an invented story, poem or play. Non-fiction is writing about real events, feelings or things.
first person	The first person pronoun is **I**. In writing it is used when the writer is writing about him or herself.
formal language/ informal language	Formal language is the speech and writing we use for people we do not know well. EXAMPLE: How do you do? Informal language is the language we use to people we know well. EXAMPLE: Hi!
gender words (masculine and feminine)	Gender words tell you about the sex of the person or animal. They can only apply to either men or women, not both. EXAMPLE: prince (masculine gender) and princess (feminine gender)

graphic novel	A story told through pictures and text.
homonym	Words with the same form but different meanings. EXAMPLES: Lucy **saw** a lion. Tom uses a **saw** to cut wood.
homophone	Words with the same sound but different meanings. EXAMPLE: **reed** and **read**
illustration	A picture, plan or diagram which is part of a text.
imperative	An imperative sentence commands or tells the reader or listener to do something. EXAMPLE: Run over there.
instructions	Instructions tell us how to do something.
introduction	The beginning of a piece of writing.
label	The words which tell us about part of a diagram, picture or map.
language	Language is what people use to share their thoughts with each other. We talk with our voices. This is spoken language. When we write we use written language.
list	A group of things or names written down one after the other.
logo	A word that names a person, feeling, thing or idea.
noun	(short for logograph) A symbol or character which represents a thing, idea or word.
persuade	To persuade is to try to make or convince someone to believe or do something.
plan	To work out what to say or write. Notes used to start a piece of writing.
plot	The plan or main facts of a story.
plural	More than one.
poem	A piece of writing which uses words and word order to create images and ideas. The lines often rhyme.
poet	A person who writes poems.
preposition	A word telling us about the place of nouns or pronouns. EXAMPLES: on, under, in
pronoun/ personal pronoun	Pronouns are words which stand in the place of a noun. Personal pronouns take the place of the names of people.
proper noun	Words that name particular people, things or feelings. Proper nouns begin with capital letters. EXAMPLES: Christmas, London, Jamilla
punctuation	A way of marking writing using full stops, capital letters, question marks etc. This helps the reader to understand.

question	A sentence which needs a response. It ends with a question mark. EXAMPLE: What is your name**?** One of four sentence types (exclamation, statement and command are the others).
question mark	The punctuation mark at the end of a question.
recount	A text which retells events for entertainment and/or information. Written or told in the past tense.
regular/ irregular verb	Verbs which form the past tense by adding -ed are regular. Others do not add -ed. They are irregular verbs.
revise	To make changes to a piece of writing to improve it.
rhyme	Words which have the same ending sounds. EXAMPLES: man, pan
sentence	A sentence is a piece of language that can stand by itself and makes sense. There are four sentence types: exclamation, question, statement and command.
setting	The time and place of events in a story.
simile	A sentence or group of words which compares something to something else. EXAMPLE: As free as a bird.
singular	One of something.
slogan	A catchy phrase or sentence which says something good about the subject of the phrase or sentence. EXAMPLE: Drinka pinta milka day!
speech marks	The inverted commas that go around what is actually said in direct speech. EXAMPLE: **"**I want my teddy,**"** said the little boy.
statement	A type of sentence which tells us something. EXAMPLE: I am called Jane. One of four sentence types (question, exclamation and command are the others).
suffixes	Endings that are added to words. A suffix can change words from singular to plural (EXAMPLE: box/box**es**); can change the tense of verbs (EXAMPLE: jump/jump**ed**) or can change the function of words (EXAMPLE: teach/teach**er**).
synonyms	Words which have the same or very close meanings. EXAMPLE: big, large, huge
tense, past tense, present tense, future tense	Tense tells us when something is happening. Past tense: something has already happened. EXAMPLE: I **sat** down. I **was sitting** down. Present tense: something is happening now. EXAMPLE: She **is sitting** down. She **sits** down. Future tense: something which will happen. EXAMPLE: She **will sit** down.
title	The heading which tells us what writing is about.
verb	A verb is a word that tells us what people are doing or being. EXAMPLE: The girls **ran** away.
verse	A part of a poem.

OXFORD
UNIVERSITY PRESS

Great Clarendon Street, Oxford, OX2 6DP

Oxford University Press is a department of the University of Oxford and furthers the University's aim of excellence in research, scholarship, and education by publishing worldwide in

Oxford New York

Athens Auckland Bangkok Bogotá Buenos Aires Calcutta Cape Town Chennai Dar es Salaam Delhi Florence Hong Kong Istanbul Karachi Kuala Lumpur Madrid Melbourne Mexico City Mumbai Nairobi Paris São Paulo Shanghai Singapore Taipei Tokyo Toronto Warsaw

and associated companies in Berlin Ibadan

Oxford is a registered trade mark of Oxford University Press

© Jane Medwell and Maureen Lewis 1999

The moral rights of the authors have been asserted

First published 1999
Reprinted 2000

British Library Cataloguing in Publication Data

Data available

Illustrated by: Sophie Grillet, Genny Haines, Alan Marks, Bethan Matthews, Shelagh McNicholas, Patricia Moffett, David Mostyn, Peter Richardson, Wendy Sinclair and Helen Wiseman

Photographs by: J. Allan Cash Ltd, Austin J. Brown Aviation Picture Library, Corel, Paul Grover, David Hempleman-Adams, Marlin Sookias, Stock Directory and Telegraph Colour Library

Acknowledgements
We are grateful to the following for permission to reproduce copyright material in this book: Anti-Cancer Council of Victoria: for 'Sid the Seagull' cartoon; John Coldwell: for 'Travelling to School' © John Coldwell 1993, first published in *A Green Poetry Paintbox*, edited by John Foster, (OUP, 1993); Pie Corbett: for 'Wings',© Pie Corbett, 1987, first published in *Another First Poetry Book*, edited by John Foster, (OUP, 1987); HarperCollins Publishers Ltd: for extracts from C.S. Lewis *The Lion, the Witch and the Wardrobe*; and for extracts and illustrations by Alan Lee from J.R.R. Tolkein: *The Hobbit* (illustrated edition, 1997); Independent Newspapers (UK) Ltd: for article 'The School Cap is Back' by Ros Wynne-Jones and accompanying photograph by Tom Pilston from *The Independent on Sunday* 19 May 1996; Laboratoires Garnier: for Ambre Solaire 'Being Sun Smart' poster and logo; Tony Mitton: for 'Many Ways to Travel', © Tony Mitton 1993, first published in *A Green Poetry Paintbox*, edited by John Foster (OUP, 1993); Oxford University Press: for extracts from Haydn Middleton: *Captain Cook* (*What's Their Story?* series); Paramount Pictures: for graphic from *Star Trek: The Next Generation – Beginnings* (published by D.C. Comics and Titan Books) © 1999 by Paramount Pictures. All rights reserved. Scholastic Inc: for extract from Katherine Applegate: *The Stranger* (*Animorphs* series); Telegraph Books: for extract from the North Pole Diary of David Hempleman-Adams reported by Robert Uhlig in *The Daily Telegraph*, 5 May 1998; A.P. Watt Ltd on behalf of The Literary Executors of the estate of H.G. Wells: for extract from H.G. Wells; *War of the Worlds*; Westwear: for 'Safe Fun in the Sun' promotional leaflet; Raymond Wilson: for 'From a Space Rocket' © Raymond Wilson 1991 *A Blue Poetry Paintbox*, edited by John Foster (OUP, 1993).

Despite every effort to trace copyright holders this has not been possible in every case. If notified, the publisher will be pleased to rectify any omission or error at the earliest opportunity.

ISBN 0 19 915551 8

Printed in Hong Kong